P9-DIF-349

Abuse and Neglect
of Handicapped Children

Abuse and Neglect of Handicapped Children

Sharon R. Morgan, Ph.D.

A College-Hill Publication

*Little, Brown and Company
Boston/Toronto/San Diego*

College-Hill Press
A Division of
Little, Brown and Company (Inc.)
34 Beacon Street
Boston, Massachusetts 02108

©1987 by Little, Brown and Company (Inc.)

All rights, including that of translation, reserved. No part of
this publication may be reproduced, stored in a retrieval system,
or transmitted in any form or by any means, electronic, mechanical,
recording, or otherwise, without the prior written permission of
the publisher.

Library of Congress Cataloging-in-Publication Data
Main entry under title:

  Morgan, Sharon R., 1942–
    Abuse and neglect of handicapped children.

    Includes index.
    1. Child abuse.   2. Handicapped children.   I. Title.
  HV6626.5.M67   1986   362.4'088054   86-24931

ISBN 0-316-58292-1

Printed in the United States of America.

You better not never tell nobody but God. It'd kill your mammy.

Dear God,
    I am fourteen years old. . . . I have always been a good girl. Maybe you can give me a sign letting me know what is happening to me.

— Alice Walker
The Color Purple

This book is dedicated to all abused and neglected children, but especially to those who are handicapped and do not even know what is happening to them.

CONTENTS

FOREWORD

The world turns and the world changes,
But one thing does not change.
The perpetual struggle of Good and Evil.
                                    —T.S. Eliot

Sadly, we are in a time when terms such as child abuse and neglect have become commonplace and all-pervasive. Occurrences of emotional, physical, and sexual abuse, which only yesterday were sensationalized by unending media coverage, are now common themes of television programs, and fiction, and nonfiction reading materials.

Enter now the handicapped child, who is protected by educational legislation, yet unprotected and as susceptible as anyone to the perversions of society. A pivotal question also remains: are these children abused because they are handicapped or are they handicapped because they have been abused? Unfortunately for many handicapped children, they do not know or cannot answer the question of why, where, or how they were abused. Lifelong debilitation can result from these episodes, which often have as much or more of a profound influence on them than the physical and/or cognitive limitations they may have acquired.

Finally, we have moved the secrets and stigma associated with abuse and neglect of handicapped children into the open with this text by Sharon Morgan. With her typical, to-the-point, easily read style, Dr. Morgan first provides the reader with background information concerning the sources of societal attitudes toward the handicapped in terms of abuse and neglect. She provides stark and revealing information of studies that document the incidences of abuse, and provides case study information that is sure to provoke and stimulate questions and responses. Dr. Morgan is straightforward in her treatment of those who are the abusers of handicapped children, sparing neither parent nor stranger. She is also fair in her discussions, pointing out that the aura of abuse has swung so wide that safeguards must be developed against witch-hunts and paranoia. An excellent recommendation of Morgan's is that we all must be our own watchdog, for the people we least expect may be the very ones we need to fear.

This text includes in its appendices checklists and documentation forms one may wish to use in trying to determine basic abuse information. Toll-free hot line phone numbers are also included for those who have more than an educational need for this material. Finally, sample reporting letters are provided, which often are difficult to write and more difficult to send.

While, for many, it appears unthinkable that individuals would take advantage of handicapped children, it really should be no surprise. The history of the handicapped in institutions bears witness to this. What should surprise us, however, is that little has been done to advocate for this population of children until recently. I believe this important and timely book by Sharon Morgan will stimulate, anger, and educate many who read it. At the least it will create feelings of uneasiness. Most important, it will send a strong message that handicapped children, like all children, are not immune from society's dark and hidden side of abuse and neglect.

Michael Bender, Ed.D.
Director of Special Education,
The Kennedy Institute;
Associate Professor of
Education and Pediatrics,
Johns Hopkins University and
School of Medicine

PREFACE

This is a book that has evolved over the last year. It started with the idea of giving Special Education teachers and administrators the information needed to identify an abused handicapped child. Several ideas that were not originally intended for the book developed as I shared the information with my university students in class, and they shared their ideas and experiences with me. As the year progressed I realized there were pressing new problems emerging that teachers and administrators needed to know about. The main concern that surfaced was the number of false accusations of abuse being brought against teachers. As I say more than once in this text, it became painfully clear that this book had to address ways for us to protect *all* of the innocents, both children and their caretakers. I hope I have accomplished this. Someday someone will undoubtedly develop ideas to solve this problem. What I have done is simply a start.

ACKNOWLEDGMENTS

Although I take full responsibility for most of what has been written here, it was Dr. Michael Bender who first recognized the need that information specifically about abuse of handicapped children was needed. I am very appreciative of the way he supported my ideas, and gave me gentle nudges of encouragement when I felt discouraged.

I am especially grateful to Jo Reinhart for the design of several of the forms in the Appendices. She has a real understanding of teachers' needs, a creative sense of what makes something work, and is a stickler for details. She spent hours correcting my grammar and punctuation, and wouldn't let me get away with making up my own jargon.

Sources of Societal Attitudes Toward the Handicapped

Child abuse is not a new phenomenon that has just become a part of the many ills of the 20th century, but is a problem that has received more attention in the 1980s than ever before. What *is* new is that mistreatment of children today is *considered* abuse.

ABUSE OF THE HANDICAPPED IN ANCIENT SOCIETIES

There are historical accounts, going far back into antiquity, that describe the many and varied ways human beings treated children who had conditions that singled them out as "different" in some way. In ancient societies abuse and murder of handicapped children was not only commonplace, but in many cultures was done because it was viewed as necessary for the general good and welfare of the community. It was done to maintain discipline, drive out evil spirits, please the gods, or make money (Durant, 1944; 1966; Kempe, 1968).

Sexual abuse and mutilation of children also has a long history; during the Greek and Roman periods many young boys were kept in bordellos and sold for sexual pleasures. A young, castrated boy could command high prices for sexual favors, so it was not extremely uncommon for some parents to castrate their children and collect large sums of money. This practice was a definite case of children who were made handicapped through abuse. Incest is not new either; it was practiced frequently in ancient cultures (Gibbon, 1899; Steinmetz & Straus, 1973).

There were three primary reasons for the abuse and murder of children in ancient societies: utilitarianism, societal value systems, and belief in the supernatural. *Utilitarianism* was based totally on a societal group's practical needs and ability to survive. If children were born with conditions so disabling that they required life-long care by someone in the group, then those children were seen as a liability to the society. Harsh environmental conditions of those ancient times placed great demands on human beings to be strong and fit so that they were able to take care of themselves and contribute to the daily living needs of the group. Simple living, in primitive times, was laborious and spirit-killing, causing people to behave in ways, that by today's standards, would be considered ruthless and barbarous (Palmer & Colton, 1967).

Children born with physical, sensory, or mental handicaps were definite liabilities to primitive societies. Not only were they unable to contribute to group efforts of providing shelter, or hunting, gathering, and farming food, their requirements for individual care would remove from the work force some able-bodied person needed for those survival tasks (Hanks & Hanks, 1948; Hebb, 1946; Rusk & Taylor, 1946).

Leaving a handicapped or chronically ill child alone to die in the forests, deserts, and mountains were some of the ways primitive societies solved that particular "problem." Other typical "solutions" to the birth of handicapped children were straightforward murder with a weapon, throwing them over cliffs or into rivers and ponds, burying them alive, or leaving them in areas where they were sure to be killed and eaten by wild beasts. Although one might imagine there had to be some parents who experienced heartbreak or feelings about such things and did not want to kill their children, group needs and expectations took precedence. Put into the perspective of the times, these child murders were all considered rather unremarkable events (Rusk & Taylor, 1946).

Societal *value systems* was another reason for child abuse and murder, and was most prominent in the Greek and Roman cultures several centuries B.C. (Durant, 1966). The Greeks and Romans valued and prized beauty, strength, and intelligence. About 355 B.C., Aristotle declared that anything imperfect should not be allowed to develop, and this dictum became law in Greece, a law that led to the death of many "imperfect" children at the hands of Greeks. Later the Romans created a similar law: they could kill their children, abandon them, or sell them into slavery, whichever they chose to do. General practice was to kill them if they were severely handicapped. Those who had more mildly handicapping conditions, or did not meet the criteria of that time for beauty, strength, and intelligence, were often abandoned or sold. Professional beggars frequently took abandoned children and, if not already handicapped, deliberately maimed them so that they could be sent to beg for money, food, or other necessities. In this way, they could be made useful for some utilitarian purpose; their differences, however, were still something to be despised. Paradoxically, if they were able to beg enough to be useful, then there must have been some people at that time who were humanitarians and somewhat sympathetic toward handicapped children (Durant, 1944).

The third reason for abusing the handicapped was belief in the *supernatural*. Some people believed that a child born with a defect was a way in which the gods or spirits punished sinful parents. In atonement for their "sins," the parents were required to put the child to death. In other societies, the child was thought to be possessed, and the parents were required to beat the child on a regular basis to drive out evil spirits. On *Holy Innocents' Day,* parents ritualistically whipped children in remembrance of the massacre of innocent children at the hands of King Herod when he heard that there was a newborn King of the Jews. This ritual began sometime after the recognition of Jesus Christ and was practiced by some sects throughout Europe and the Middle East (Durant, 1944; Kempe, 1968).

In other cultures, a child born with a defect was believed to be a sign from the gods that they wanted the child returned to them, explanations ranging from the notion that the parents did not, for whatever reason, yet deserve a child, to the idea that the parents were being honored and upon them was bestowed the high privilege of giving a child to the gods or spirits. However it was explained, the babies were used as sacrifices in public ceremonies (Durant, 1966; Hanks & Hanks, 1948; Hebb, 1946; Kanner, 1964; Lippman, 1972).

Historical accounts of how children and adults with emotional disturbances were treated vary greatly, in that different cultural groups and societies had extreme responses to them. If a group thought the disturbed possessed evil spirits then, out of fear, they either murdered them, treated them brutally, or just avoided them. If a group thought the disturbed were possessed of strong spirits, either bad or good, then in order to protect themselves and bring great power to their society, they gave them exalted positions, such as: witch doctors, medicine men or women, high priests or priestesses, fortune tellers, and shamans. Some tribes of Indians saw them as bringing good luck and would take them on hunting trips, have them stand in the fields while crops were being planted, or bring them to the tepee of a woman about to give birth (Andrews, 1982; Durant, 1944, 1966; Graybill & Boesen, 1976; Hebb, 1946; Kauffman, 1980).

ABUSE OF THE HANDICAPPED IN SOCIETIES TODAY

Why individuals with differences are abused by their own kind is a question that some scientists have tried to explain with a theory referred to as the *principle of genetic reductionism*. Basically, this means that animals, in general, reject any of their own kind that are deviant; in other words, it is a natural-born inclination in all animals to cull out those that are defective. Human beings, because they are also animals, are only doing what is natural when they abuse or kill other human beings who are defective. This theory has been debunked as simply myth by both animal and social psychologists (Scheerer, 1954). There are numerous examples of the various behaviors of different animal species toward their own disabled. (Korbin, 1977; Maisel, 1953; Scheerer, 1954; Wright, 1983). The following is just a sampling:

- Wolves do not attack or avoid physically disabled wolves.
- Sharks will attack, kill, and eat another disabled shark.
- Baboons are brutal toward other baboons with physical deviations.
- Chimpanzees will not attack a handicapped chimpanzee of their group.
- Goldfish with missing fins are accepted by other goldfish.

What of human beings? The literature demonstrates that there is just as much variability among humans as among the lower animals. (Hanks & Hanks, 1948; Hebb, 1946; Korbin, 1977; Maisel, 1953; Ogbu, 1981; Wright, 1983). Following are a few examples from various tribes of people around the world:

- Siriono Indians will abandon or kill those who are sick or physically disabled.
- The Chagga of Africa believe crippled people satisfy evil spirits so that others can be normal; therefore, no one dare

harm children or adults who are handicapped in any way, no matter how severe their condition.

- The Navajo Indians derive great satisfaction from sadistic humor that ridicules those in the tribe who are handicapped, and they frequently imitate them in public and give them cruel nicknames.

- The Sema Nagas have declared it taboo to abuse or kill anyone with any handicapping condition.

- The Dieri Aborigines of Australia kill deformed children.

- The Palaung, a clan living on an island in the Far East, consider it very lucky to have extra fingers or toes, and extremely lucky to have a hare-lip.

People with congenital as opposed to acquired deformities are sometimes treated differently: the Wogeo of New Guinea bury alive children born with obvious deformities, but give loving care to children who might become handicapped or ill later in life. In general, children who are different, deformed, handicapped, or disabled in some way are either feared and hated or feared and revered. Not too frequently are they simply treated in an ordinary way, although there are a few examples: the Ponape Indians treat physically handicapped and emotionally disturbed children just as they treat normal children; the Azande tribe never kill abnormal children nor do those children ever lack the love of their parents (Andrews, 1982; deSilva, 1981; Graybill & Boesen, 1976; Hanks & Hanks, 1948; Hebb, 1946; Korbin, 1977; Lippman, 1972; Maisel, 1953; Ogbu, 1981; Wright, 1983).

Though we seem to have improved in our attitudes and willingness to help those who are less fortunate, we still have much more growing to do as a species. All of the horrible ways that handicapped infants and children were treated in ancient societies have not disappeared entirely and continue in the 20th century. At the very worst, some are still being abused emotionally, physically, and sexually, and some are still being murdered (Meier, 1985; Morgan, 1985; Rush, 1980; Schultz & Jones, 1983). At the very least, many children with handicapping conditions still experience devaluation, dehumanization, underprivileged status, stereotyping, rejection, and discrimination (Wright, 1983).

Most mistreatment of children with handicapping conditions is perpetrated by parents or other family members. In personal interviews with abusive parents, some have defended what they do based on such old axioms as, "spare the rod and spoil the child." Other parents have abused their children by hiding them in barns or basements, nearly starving them. Others who follow certain religious beliefs still beat their handicapped children because they continue to live by the ancient biblical adage, " . . . and the sins of the father shall be visited upon the son . . . "; that is, they mistreat their children and keep them hidden because of their religious beliefs. They feel they have been "sinful" in some perceived way and the child's handicapped condition reflects that sin and causes them embarrassment.

While we have not been able to learn with any degree of certainty why lower-form animals treat disabled members of their species in the various ways they do, we have learned some of the reasons why there is variability in human behavior toward the disabled and handicapped. The three main reasons mentioned earlier that influence abusive behavior toward the handicapped in ancient societies persist in societies today.

In the past as well as today, those who have handicapping conditions are never viewed as *just* normal. Normality in all cultures is basically defined as what is usual or what the majority are like. In fact, differences, disabilities, deformities, and handicapping conditions exist in all species and have been in existence through the ages in all societies and cultures. They have always been with us and they always will be. We would have no need of discussions, special studies, elaborate organizations, laws, and intricate regulations to protect those with conditions that the majority do not have if we were not still so bound-up with a utilitarian philosophy, our value systems, and beliefs in the supernatural. It is interesting to speculate how different things would be if we took the stance that normal is what *is*; if it exists, it is normal.

If there is any doubt about our clinging to past influences, we only need to look at the current controversies regarding the handicapped raging in the educational, ecclesiastical, and medical communities, legislative forums, and judicial courts; a close look at these various arguments can reveal influences that always seem to have been with humankind. At least one example of the arguments under discussion in society today follows:

EDUCATIONAL. Should we expend great amounts of money attempting to educate or train handicapped children? What purpose does it serve when they will never become fully contributing members of society, especially when the monies spent could be providing more for normal and gifted children who are more certain to make some return to society for its investment. *(utilitarianism)*.

ECCLESIASTICAL. What was the deity's (deities') intentions for the birth of such children? There is at least one Christian sect that still believes the birth of a handicapped child is a blessing and a sign from God that the parents are more good and more holy than those who do not have handicapped children *(the supernatural)*.

MEDICAL. Should we be using extraordinary means to keep alive severely deformed and critically ill children when they will never be able to experience the quality of life of normal human beings *(value systems)*?

It is up to the legislators and judiciaries to try to keep these three reasons for all constituents in balance, but it should not be forgotten that the legislation they propose and the rulings they pass are influenced, in some way, by those same three reasons that influence others. Public servants are also only human, after all, and subject to different philosophies, value systems, and supernatural beliefs.

At this juncture, the reader is reminded that the author is not providing a personal opinion, commentary or judgment about any of the above-mentioned controversies. Rather, observations are being made to draw attention to the fact that our present is still, in some ways, inextricably intertwined with our past. Perhaps what distinguishes the things some people do today from what they did in ancient times in various cultures is that we discuss, question, and, when able, change our customs, habits, behaviors, and laws in a more cognizant, responsible manner.

CHAPTER 2

Defining Child Abuse
and Neglect

In 1974 Congress passed the Child Abuse Prevention and Treatment Act [Public Law 93–247, 93rd Congress, Senate 1191, 1974], which is federal law and provides a basic definition of child abuse. It reads as follows:

> The physical or mental injury, sexual abuse, negligent treatment, or maltreatment of a child under the age of eighteen by a person who is responsible for the child's welfare under circumstances which indicate the child's health or welfare is harmed or threatened thereby.

Although the federal definition is fairly general in nature, it does provide an "umbrella" law and a starting point for states to work with. It prescribes three prerequisites that, from a legal standpoint, distinguish child abuse as a crime that is substantively and qualitatively different from the crimes of assault and battery, or rape. The first prerequisite is age: the individual must be under 18 to qualify as a minor (child), which distinguishes this crime from other crimes (assault and battery, rape) already covered by law. The second is that the injury is nonaccidental (i.e., abuse): it was a deliberate act with the intent of causing damage. The third prerequisite is that the abuse has been perpetrated by a caretaker (i.e., child abuse), as opposed to a stranger, in which case the crime would be covered by a law pertaining to assault and battery, indecent behavior with a child, or rape. In addition, the caretaker clause allows for criminal punishment of other behaviors in which a stranger has, morality aside, no legal responsibility; i.e., neglect, abandonment, and emotional abuse. Caretakers, in the eyes of the law, include parents, stepparents, foster parents, guardians, baby-sitters, day-care center attendants, teachers, and other school personnel. In other words, anyone who is responsible for taking care of a child, temporarily or otherwise.

Other definitions of child abuse range from commission—willfully inflicting physical injury on a child (Kempe and Kempe, 1976), to omission—wasting a child's potential by failing to provide conditions necessary for optimal development (Gil, 1976). Child abuse, then, includes intentional acts of commission or omission on the part of the caretaker that result in physical injury or emotional damage to a child (Junewicz, 1983).

Mental health professionals recognize several types of abuse: nonaccidental physical injury, physical neglect, sexual molestation, and emotional abuse and neglect. Since the definition of abuse includes obstructing a child's optimal development, there are strong implications for professionals working with children, particularly in educational settings (Morgan, 1985). Obstruction of a child's optimal development is something that teachers need to be keenly concerned about since teaching the developing child is the lifeblood of their work (Gil, 1976).

In the past, physicians, psychologists, and social workers reported nearly all child abuse cases. Child abuse was a mental health issue that was then, almost exclusively, an area to be studied and researched by other professionals, but this is no longer the case. With annual abuse figures as high as they are, it is safe to guess that virtually every teacher will, at some time or another, have an abused child of some type in the classroom. All states have laws regarding child abuse, reporting procedures, and the responsibilities of certain adults who are aware of any type of abuse that is occurring. By law, most school personnel are required to report suspected cases of child abuse, although there are some unusual exceptions. In one state, for example, school administrators do not have to report; in another state, school nurses do not have to report; in four states, counselors do not have to report; in two states, school social workers do not have to report; and in three states, teachers do not have to report (Camblin & Prout, 1983). Even if someone works in a place where there are no legal repercussions, these things should not be ignored just because the law says that a person is permitted to ignore abuse. Few teachers would turn their backs on an abused child, no matter how temporarily unpleasant, uncomfortable, or difficult it may make their own lives for becoming involved.

Child abuse affects us as a nation because it destroys children who are the nation's resources. Accounts of abuse as children are reported repeatedly by delinquents, adult criminals, adolescent drug offenders, and prostitutes (Tarter, Hegedus, Winsten, & Alterman, 1984). Agencies and governmental committees believe the financial cost to society in dealing with the results of child abuse are astronomical. Most importantly, the cost in human suffering and wasted potential cannot even be calculated: Money and cost to the nation is inconsequential in comparison to human suffering, and wasted lives and potential. Those who physically survive the abuse inflicted on them as children often suffer consequences for the rest of their lives (Morgan, 1985).

It is extremely important for school personnel to understand that there *can* be legal penalties for those who fail to report because all 50 states have some law for the criminal prosecution of child abusers; not to report is something akin to withholding evidence. There are specific legal definitions of what constitutes child abuse that differs from state to state. All educators need to become familiar with their state definitions and laws. For instance, all states have clear laws about physical and sexual abuse, but when it comes to emotional neglect and abuse, the issue is less clear and laws less definite. At the time of this writing there are seven states that do not require school personnel to report emotional neglect, three states that do not require the reporting of abandonment, one state that does not require the reporting of children at risk for abuse, and one state that does not require reporting "general maltreatment." In addition, only three states do require that exploitation of children be reported (Camblin & Prout, 1983). Though all school personnel are not always required to report all types of abuse in all 50 states, each state does have at least one statewide agency that is required by law to receive and investigate reports of *any* type of child abuse.

EMOTIONAL ABUSE

Children who suffer emotional abuse are subjected to mental and emotional torment that is somewhat difficult to describe and define. Although there have been attempts to define emotional abuse, it is still very difficult to describe what is actually happening to a child in such a way that abuse is clearly evident. In contrast to neglect and physical or sexual abuse, this type of abuse is nebulous because the outward signs are hazy, indistinct, and obscure. Unless people in the schools are very knowledgable on this subject, and few professionals truly are, and really know the child and family, then emotional abuse, in large part, goes unnoticed (Dean, 1979).

Emotional abuse is, in some ways, analogous to prejudice, which has insidious consequences. It is stealthily treacherous because it is usually inconspicuous to outsiders but has a grave, injurious effect on the self-esteem and emotional life of a person. Even adults who experience prejudice find it difficult to describe to people who have not experienced prejudice what has or is actually happening to them. They cannot go to someone and say that so-and-so beat them up, spit in their face, or pulled their hair. Some types of discrimination or prejudice are so subtle that people who have tried to describe them will tell you that, when they repeat what actually transpired, it sounds almost silly and trivial (Morgan, 1985).

Emotional abuse is often more subtle than most cases described in the literature, so people really cannot be blamed when the problem is not recognized; it is difficult to identify. Even attorneys have trouble prosecuting cases of emotional abuse, which is a strong signal that it is not easy to identify and define in concrete terms. If lawyers, who can nearly always make something out of nothing, have trouble with this issue, then it becomes next to impossible for other professionals to provide effective help.

The National Committee for Prevention of Child Abuse (1983) defines emotional abuse as including:

> . . . excessive, aggressive, or unreasonable parental demands that place expectations on a child beyond his or her capabilities. Emotional abuse can show itself in constant and persistent teasing, belittling, or verbal attacks. Emotional abuses also include failures to provide the psychological nurturance necessary for a child's psychological growth and development—no love, no care, no support, no guidance [p. 5].

Some of the actions parents take that constitute emotional abuse have been described by Garbarino and Garbarino (1984). There are parents who knowingly refuse to allow attachment and bonding to take place between them and their infants. They frequently punish their child for showing signs of positive normal behavior, such as walking, talking, smiling, exploring their environment, exhibiting signs of good self-esteem, and for trying to form social relationships and friendships outside the immediate family.

This certainly defines the problem well—that *is* exactly what emotional abuse is all about! Unfortunately, however, these parental behaviors cannot always be seen because they are usually perpetrated in secrecy. Dean (1979) has attempted to better clarify the legalities by describing several court cases that have been adjudicated. Legal interpretations of abuse may vary from court to court but most courts are reluctant to get involved unless the effects of emotional abuse are very clear and unusually extreme. Of the three court cases successfully presented, all involved one or more of the following characteristics:

> an act that in itself is sufficient to establish abuse; differential treatment of one child in the family; and [*word added*] a reduction in the child's functioning that can be linked to abusive treatment (p. 19).

Dean states that when preparing for court, it is necessary to document which of the characteristics are present and show that the emotional abuse has had a detrimental effect on the child. She gives several examples of emotional abuse that reached the courts. One involved a child who had to wear a sign on herself wherever she went that told of the wrong-doing she had done; another case was of an adolescent who had to stand in his front yard in diapers as punishment; and the third was of a child who was the family scapegoat, and whose mistreatment was both obvious and observable.

> These cases involved extreme public humiliation and the courts ruled that a child has a right to reasonable and just discipline in the privacy of the home. Subjecting a child to public scorn was not considered reasonable or positive discipline (p. 19).

It is good, of course, that these cases reached the courts where intervention could take place for those children. What is distressing about these rulings is the courts' usage of the language, "in the privacy of the home," so that when it comes to emotional abuse, in effect, the courts have said parents can treat their children as they please as long as it is done in private. It is doubtful that the children who are emotionally abused in less obvious and concrete ways would feel particularly comforted and satisfied by that ruling.

Educators should take particular note of the wording in the ruling handed down by the courts, " . . . reasonable and just discipline. . . ." Public scorn and humiliation can be grounds for prosecution of emotional abuse. Legal repercussion is *not* the most important reason to give pause and greater consideration to the ways in which children are disciplined in the schools but, for those who may not understand anything else, it is a great incentive to learn and use more effective, humane methods of behavior management.

Signs of Emotional Abuse

Before the National Committee for Prevention of Child Abuse distributed material calling attention to the types of abuse, some local child protective agencies developed definitions of their own that were based upon the research of the most noted authorities on the subjects. Rarely was emotional abuse mentioned. One local child protective agency created a paper for their newly hired social workers, which discussed physical abuse, physical neglect, and refers to what they termed "emotional neglect." Surprisingly enough, sexual abuse was not mentioned at all. For "emotional neglect" the agency listed certain signs to observe in children such as moodiness, being withdrawn, aggressiveness, difficulties in school adjustment, temper tantrums, and stuttering. The symptoms sound like those that could be observed in a child experiencing any number of problems or crises. It also states that if these symptoms are observed, the child is undoubtedly "emotionally neglected" and is probably being subjected to family friction, marital discord, or is rejected. It also warns that a child will be "emotionally neglected" if one or both of the parents is disturbed by neurosis or psychosis.

Another paper from a local agency also listed signs of "emotional neglect," with the intention of alerting social workers. This paper posed such questions as:

Is the child loved or hated?

Is the child constantly scolded and scapegoated?

Is the child constantly discouraged?

Is there excessive alcoholic consumption in the family?

Does the excessive use of alcohol cause behaviors that create severe family conflicts?

Does the child appear lost in the family setting?

Is there a stepparent who is jealous or who resents the child?

Is the child rejected?

These are parental behaviors that are related to emotional abuse as we understand it today. Social workers who have access to the home are usually in a better position to determine the existence of these behaviors. It is more difficult for teachers and other school professionals to make such determinations unless the behavior of the child at school is obvious and serious enough to warrant a home visit. Even then, teachers typically do not and often are not allowed to visit unannounced; therefore, when they do visit the home they commonly find the parents on their best behavior (Dean, 1979; Foreman & Seligman, 1983; Junewicz, 1983; Kavanagh, 1982; Lourie & Stefano, 1978; Whiting, 1976).

Drawing from the literature that exists on emotional abuse (Garbarino & Garbarino, 1984; Lourie & Stefano, 1978; Money, 1982; Morgan, 1985; Moss & Moss, 1984; Mulford, 1958; Rohner, 1975; Straker & Johnson, 1981; Whiting, 1978), there are a number of signs or characteristics of children who have been emotionally abused:

1. Self-destructive behavior

2. Apathy, depression, and withdrawal

3. Academic failure

4. Developmental delays

5. Hyperactivity, tantrums, and conduct disorders

6. Pseudo-maturity

7. Lacks trust

8. Rigid, compulsive, and disorganized

9. Feelings of inadequacy and poor self-esteem

10. Role reversal—the child takes care of the parent

11. Excessive fantasy

12. Fearful and hypervigilent

13. Lacks creativity

14. Poor peer relations or peer dependence

15. Lacks familial attachment

16. Gender confusion

17. Lacks empathy

18. Excessive anxiety and night terrors

19. Oblivious to hazards and risks

Obviously these are not exclusively symptoms of emotional abuse; they appear again as symptoms of children physically and sexually abused. There are only so many ways a child can respond to tragedies and crisis-ridden lives. The point is to keep emphasizing symptoms so that professionals are alerted to children who are in danger; the child must first be identified.

PHYSICAL ABUSE AND NEGLECT

The National Committee for Prevention of Child Abuse (1983) estimates that in the United States alone, approximately 1 million children every year are abused by their parents, guardians, or someone who has the responsibility of providing care for a child. Children with handicapping conditions are included in these figures, which the Committee considers to be a conservative estimate. The abuse of children by their caretakers is recognized as a major national health problem. Depending on the source, the figures of children who die as a direct result of physical abuse and neglect range from 2,000 to 5,000 per year.

This type of abuse is readily identifiable by the characteristics of physical trauma suffered by the child. More common evidence includes: bruises, contusions, lacerations, broken bones, burns, and missing hair that has been pulled from the scalp. This type of abuse is not easily hidden. Neglect can occur in a variety of ways as well: lack of enough to eat, inappropriate food, drink, or medicine, improper and inadequate clothing for weather conditions, inappropriate treatment of injuries, lack of medical care, a lack of concern or taking responsibility to educate the child by providing basic school materials or seeing that he or she gets to school, and the ultimate neglect—abandonment.

Signs of Physical Abuse and Neglect

Rather than present a long list of the obvious physical signs of neglect and abuse, it is equally important to discuss behavioral and psychological signs of abuse; they are the indicators most often misunderstood and overlooked. An examination of the research shows that there are at least four major personality styles that are consistently seen in the abused and neglected child: passiveness, aggressiveness, regressiveness, and interpersonal relationship deficits (Bakan, 1971; Elmer, 1967; Galdston, 1974; Greene, 1974; Justice & Justice, 1976; Kinard, 1979; Martin & Rodeheffer, 1976; Morgan, 1979; Morse, Sahler, & Friedman, 1970; Ounsted, Oppenheimer, & Lindsay, 1974).

The Passive Child

Galdston (1974) likened the passive child to an adult who was suffering from "shell shock." Ounsted et al. (1974) uses the term "frozen watchfulness," which is seen as a child's attempt to cope with unpredictable parental behavior, when basic trust and a consistent environment has not been established. Older children may not withdraw to the extent of frozen watchfulness, but they may become extremely passive and withdrawn. They show little initiative and avoid attracting attention to themselves, making few demands, if any, and trying to act as if they are not part of the environment. Typically, these children do not take action until they are fairly certain of what the reaction of the adults might be. Rarely, do they express their own thoughts or ideas since they have learned this can be very dangerous in an abusive environment (Court, 1974; Justice & Justice, 1976).

Another behavior associated with the passive child is termed hypervigilance, which is the intent watching of adults in the environment and becoming acutely sensitive to their mood changes. This is a sharply developed perceptual skill that these children use out of necessity to avoid further attacks and injury (Martin & Rodeheffer, 1976).

Since abused children are only appreciated when they meet parental needs and expectations, they often take on, along with hypervigilance, pseudoadult behaviors that frequently result in a role-reversal between child and parent. The children become their parents' caretakers, both emotionally and physically. This gives them the appearance of being mature, charming, considerate, and sensitive to the moods and wishes of others (Court, 1974; Davoren, 1974; Justice & Justice, 1976; Martin & Rodeheffer, 1976).

Passivity tends to be cited in studies as a major distinguishing feature of the abused child. Because of the characteristics of passive children, they frequently go unrecognized as needing help even though they may be more at risk psychologically than their aggressive peers, because they are not identified as children with problems (Muir, 1976).

The Aggressive Child

Severe physical punishment has been associated with a lowering of the aggressive threshold and appears to be a major factor in the development of such deviant behaviors as anger and violence, distractability, social ineptness, impulsivity, and the anti-authoritarian attitudes so prevalent among delinquents. It has been noted that the hostility of battered children often gets channeled into inappropriate and destructive patterns such as acting-out their anger on others. This acting-out may take the form of stealing money so that they can buy gifts that can be used to buy friendships (Bakan, 1971; Curtis, 1974; Greene, 1974; Kent, 1976; Welsh, 1976a, 1976b).

Aggression may not always be focused toward others. Often, as these children get older, they develop self-hatred, blaming themselves for their parents' mistreatment and then turning their aggression inward. This self-hatred can be seen in passive-aggressive behavior, which is used by the child in an attempt to hold on to some sense of integrity in a family where the youngster's rights as a person are constantly denied. Passive aggressiveness allows the child to defy authority without confronting a person directly and openly. An example of such behavior is the child who acquiesces verbally to some request but then does just the opposite, and, when confronted, acts incompetent or as if the request was misunderstood (Bakan, 1971; Martin & Rodeheffer, 1976; Welsh, 1976a, 1976b; Galdston, 1974).

It has been observed that physically abused children go through an aggressive phase as they come out of their extreme passivity. These aggressive behaviors have been suggested as a way of testing new relationships and also reinforcing their own negative self-concept and internal guilt.

Many of these children seem to have poor impulse control, which is understandable when it is realized that they come from abusive environments where the parents also have poor impulse control. This leaves the child with little else to model (Curtis, 1974; Elmer, 1967). It can certainly be looked at in two ways: that the battered child's aggression, hostility, and anger is so intense that it comes out indiscriminately directed at peers; or that the child has identified with the parental model; or both.

Repeatedly in the literature, battered children who are especially aggressive are believed to provoke their own abuse and neglect. They are identified early-on as troublemakers and begin to encounter serious difficulties with peers and other adults who may become abusive in return (George & Main, 1979). More knowledgable professionals quickly recognize this assaultive, aggressive behavior as the child's cry for help. The schools need to be aware of an abused child's reason for bad behavior so that they do not exacerbate, with corporal punishment, the abuse the child already receives at home (Morgan, 1976).

The Regressive Child

Some children regress to inappropriate behaviors as a way of coping with an abusive environment. These children frequently become enuretic, cry easily and often, masturbate, thumbsuck, act immature, and withdraw into fantasy worlds. Their behavior is often paradoxical in that they tend to be overly dependent while at the same time withdrawing from even a kind human touch. Their regressive behavior seems to be an attempt to gain sympathy by exaggerating their helplessness (Greene, 1974; Justice & Justice, 1976; Muir, 1976).

Interpersonal Relationship Deficits

The abused and battered child has been characterized as lonely, asocial, and joyless; often isolated from friends, having shallow parental relationships, they exhibit superficially friendly attitudes toward adults (Morgan, 1979). Galdston (1974) believes that the quantity and quality of gratification the physically abused child experiences with other human beings is so deficient that the ego skills needed to relate to others and progress to more mature levels is prevented from developing. As a defense, many children in abusing homes are forced to restrict various autonomous ego functions, which results in withdrawal and inhibition of personal drives and impulses. The inconsistency of an abusive environment also makes the development of trust nearly impossible. Since people in the home are always changing in unpredictable ways, the child must keep changing behaviors to adapt. This lack of consistency precludes learning appropriate interpersonal relationship skills, since what is acceptable one day probably will not be acceptable another (Kinard, 1979; Martin & Rodeheffer, 1976; Ounsted et al., 1974).

Finally, these children have poor self-concepts and practically no sense of autonomy. This is a direct result of not being valued unless they are meeting the needs and expectations of the adults in their environments. Impaired interpersonal relationships only serve to reinforce the child's negative self-concept and perpetuate the cycle (Galdston, 1974).

SEXUAL ABUSE

Not all of the types of sexual mistreatment recognized by mental health professionals are considered criminal offenses, and not all are listed in many of the states' child abuse and neglect statutes. A child can be sexually abused in a variety of ways other than actual physical contact; ways that can leave permanent psychological and emotional scars.

Most people are aware of sexual molestations that include touching and fondling a child's genitals, vaginal, anal, or oral intercourse or rape, attempted but incompleted intercourse, incest, prostitution, and the use of children in pornography. Children can also be considered sexually abused, from a mental health standpoint, without actually being physically molested. Such abuse comprises the acts of exposing youngsters to the sexually explicit behavior of adults with the intention of arousing or shocking them, obscene phone calls, verbal insinuation or seductiveness, voyeurism, and exhibitionism (Jones, 1982; Summit & Kryso, 1978; Woodling, 1981). It could be considered sexual abuse when an adult lewdly stares at children to the extent that it causes discomfort, worry, uneasiness, fear, and intimidation; any use of children in media or theatrical productions that involves them in sexually explicit or sexually subtle activities, regardless of parental consent or intent, and whether or not the parents or a paid professional believes the child has the ability to understand and cope, cognitively and emotionally (Morgan, 1985).

Incidence Figures

The problem of sexual abuse of children is of unknown national dimensions. On a daily basis, particularly since the McMartin preschool case in Manhattan Beach, California, the news and research literature points to the probability of an enormous national incidence of sexual abuse many times greater than ever expected and of greater incidence than even the reports of physical batterings. On national television and at the Senate Children's Caucus hearing on child sexual abuse, Senator Paula Hawkins of Florida, herself sexually abused as a child, stated, "My fear is that the number of children who have this problem may be in the millions." We have no way of knowing the actual figures, but it could, indeed, be well in excess of a million (DeJong, 1982; Khan, 1983; Koch, 1980; Shah, 1982; Sheehy, 1984; Williams, 1981).

Reliable data really are not available, partly due to secrecy and the taboos that surround this issue and prevent the reporting of such cases, particularly when incest is the offense. Sexual crimes against children may be reported to law-enforcement agencies, but never reach the state abuse agency to be included in their statistics. Also, not all states categorize sexual abuse separately from physical abuse (Khan, 1983; Merrill, 1975; National Committee for Prevention of Child Abuse, 1983; Williams, 1981).

In the United States, the estimates may range from 45,000 incidents a year to the incredible possibility of an excess of 1 million cases annually, depending on the source of information. Another factor that clouds the incidence issue is who gets reported. Some report figures for only girls and do not include sexual attacks on boys; others report on both girls and boys. Some have an age limitation, reporting only cases that involve children under age 14; others report cases involving youngsters up to the age of 16. National studies reveal that 1 in 5 cases of sexual abuse happens to children under the age of seven, but those in the most danger of being abused are between the ages of 8 and 12. Even infants and toddlers are subjected to sexual abuse: this has been determined by medical examinations. Finally, for the most part, child prostitutes, victims of pornography, and victims of nontouching offenses are excluded in many estimates (Sheehy, 1984; Williams, 1981; Williams, 1983).

Until recently, our society has closed its eyes to the needs of children who have been sexually abused. At one time, some law-enforcement officials had a rule that children could not be believed until they were at least 12 years of age (Sheehy, 1984). Even among psychiatrists and psychologists, sexual abuse has been clouded over by hasty conclusions and misinformation, partly because of the reliance on Freudian theory, which proposes that many children (girls in particular) fantasize such events. When the research is reviewed, it is strikingly evident that this is a *real* problem needing the full attention of professionals in the schools.

Symptoms of Sexual Abuse

There are a number of physical and behavioral symptoms indicative of sexual abuse (Fontana & Schneider, 1978; Giarretto, 1982; Jones, 1982; Morgan, 1984, 1985; Mrazek, 1980; National

Committee for Child Abuse, 1983; Shamray, 1980; Swift, 1979; Williams, 1981). These include:

1. Physical injuries to the genital area, such as vaginal tears

2. Sexually transmitted diseases

3. Difficulty urinating

4. Discharges from the penis or vagina

5. Pregnancy

6. Fear or aggressive behavior towards adults, especially their own parents

7. Sexual self-consciousness

8. Sexual promiscuity and acting-out

9. Inability to establish appropriate relationships with peers

10. Running away, stealing, and using alcohol or drugs

11. Withdrawal, regressive behavior, or behavior that makes the child look retarded

12. Seems to use school as a sanctuary by coming early and not wanting to go home

13. Complaints of frequent nightmares

14. Indirect hints that they are afraid to go home or afraid of someone in particular at home

Any information children relate that involves sexual encounters should be taken seriously. There are known cases where children have not been accurate or truthful about such matters, but, in general, children are telling the truth.

Appendix A, form 1, contains a checklist of symptoms and signs that children manifest and are indicative of abuse. It is necessary to keep accurate, dated information for the purpose of filing reports to the appropriate agency that will be making an investigation.

CHAPTER 3

The Question of
Cause and Effect

In April of 1974, The Council for Exceptional Children adopted a resolution that recognized abused and neglected children as *exceptional children* (Nazzaro, 1974). Some attention has been given to the relationship between abuse and handicapping conditions but this area has not been well researched. We know, of course, that children with handicapping conditions are not exempt from abuse. From what is available in the literature, it appears that the handicapped are neglected and abused physically, sexually, and emotionally in at least the same proportion as the population of "normal" children. In other words, according to the research that has been done, it appears on the surface that children with handicapping conditions are neglected and abused no more or no less than children who do not have handicapping conditions (Herrenkohl & Herrenkohl, 1979; Kline, 1982; Souther, 1984; Trout, 1983).

We do know that some children, who at one time were pursuing a normal course of physical and psychosocial development, have acquired handicapping conditions as a result of abuse. For instance, some children have become emotionally disturbed; some have neurological disorders because of head injuries resulting from abuse; and some children are mentally retarded because of neglect or abuse (Brandwein, 1973; Caffey, 1974; Chase & Martin, 1970; Rose & Hardman, 1981). In fact, the whole range of disabilities can, for some children, be directly attributed to the different types of neglect and abuse they have suffered; we are not certain, however, of the precise number.

Infants born with certain kinds of problems or differences in personality seem especially vulnerable to physical abuse. It has been suggested that there is a probability that some children may be born with a predisposition to abuse. Some prominent characteristics of abused infants that are most frequently reported are colick, asthma, eczema, sleep disorders, irritability, and excessive crying (Martin & Beezley, 1974; Ounsted et al., 1974).

Other researchers found that a high percentage of abused infants evidenced aberrations in social interactions and general functioning in the year prior to the abuse incident. There appears to be a strong correlation between psychological and behavioral problems and abuse (Gil, 1969; Soeffing, 1975). Kline and Christiansen (1975) found that aggressiveness and withdrawal were the most commonly observed trait in abused children. Specific behaviors they found to be associated with physical abuse were: fear, poor social relationships, destructiveness, aggressiveness, and withdrawal. Most abused children in this study exhibited one or more of these traits.

In a similar study, Kent (1976) found many of the same characteristics, such as poor peer relationships, tantrums, excessive disobedience, withdrawal, and aggression. Kent's subjects were characterized by observers as being either more aggressive or disobedient, and having more problems with peer relationships than children who were neglected or nonabused. The question of cause and effect was first raised by Sandgrund, Gaines, and Green (1974) when they found in their study that there were almost 10 times as many children with IQs below 70 in the abused group than in the nonabused group.

In many cases, to ask the question of whether children are abused because they are handicapped, or handicapped because they are abused, is something akin to the old question of which came first—the chicken or the egg. We know this much for certain: some children *are* abused because they are handicapped, and some children *are* handicapped as a result of having been abused (Frodi, 1981; Herrenkohl, Herrenkohl, & Egolf, 1983; Milner & Wimberley, 1980). The next section attempts to sort out those studies that seem to make a case for one side or the other of the issue.

HANDICAPPED BECAUSE THEY HAVE BEEN ABUSED

Before 1960, a few scattered reports concerned with child abuse could be found in the literature. Kempe, Silverman, Steele, Droegemueller, & Silver (1962) first called attention to the problem in a study of over 300 cases of abuse in the United States. It was reported in this study that 11 percent of these children died and 28 percent had permanent injuries because of the abuse.

In 1967, Elmer concluded that 90 percent of the children in her study who were abused showed evidence of residual damage, while only 10 percent were free of intellectual, physical, and emotional problems. Ten years later Elmer (1977) conducted a follow-up study on the traumatized infants, and found that 47 percent of those who had been abused were less-than-average achievers in school, and 24 percent were poor to very poor in neurologic integrity.

Others (Kempe et al., 1962) found that approximately 55 percent of the children who had been physically abused had IQs of less than 80. Some researchers have not found incidence rates of mental retardation quite as high, although the figures are still of large proportion. For instance, Martin (1976) reported 33 percent of his subjects had IQs of below 80 and 43 percent were neurologically damaged. The children in his study with normal intellect did, however, show delay in learning how to speak.

The thousands of severely and profoundly retarded children are sufficient documentation of the relationship between brain damage and mental retardation. One well-known fact is that the majority of these children sustained injury to the brain prenatally (before birth) or perinatally (shortly before or shortly after birth). What is not as clear is the actual number of cases of postnatal head trauma resulting from abuse (Brandwein, 1973). Rose and Hardman (1981) believe we can expect in any group of physically abused children that from 20 percent to 50 percent will suffer brain damage ranging from mild to severe.

Other researchers (Caffey, 1974; Elmer, 1967) have reported a high incidence of brain injury among abused children. Particularly notable is that the majority of these injuries are subdural hematomas (blood and cerebrospinal fluid putting pressure against the brain), which can prevent the brain from growing and cause mental retardation. Very often they are caused by the whiplash shaking of infants (Caffey, 1974).

According to other investigators (Chase & Martin, 1970; Elmer, 1967), mental retardation among abused children is not *only* related to physical abuse. They have indicated that there are a combination of factors involved, such as head traumas, abusive environments, and malnutrition. Malnutrition, being one of the most common forms of neglect and abuse, can cause permanent mental retardation, particularly if it occurs during the first year of life. In terms of development, the first year of life is the most critical and it is also the time when children are most vulnerable and in danger of being abused.

During early infancy, permanent, irreparable damage to the nervous system can occur as a result of malnutrition and neglect, and depress the adaptive and intellectual capacity of children. The impact of neglect on neural development is most critical during the early years of life (conception to 6 years of age). During this period the brain achieves 90 percent of its growth. The results of neglect and malnutrition during these years cannot be corrected after the child reaches school age. Neglected children inadequately integrate intersensory information. There is additional evidence that mild malnutrition in older children may reduce their ability to focus, orient, or sustain interest in learning tasks. Perceptual deficiencies, fatigue, and irritability have also been documented in neglected children (Martin, Beezley, Conway, & Kempe, 1974).

The environment can contain elements of deprivation, neglect, undernutrition, or forms of unstable family functioning that can lead to specific types of handicapping conditions. Neglect can have a detrimental effect on the child's development even without malnutrition, deprivation, parental disturbance, or low socioeconomic status (Martin, 1976; Martin & Rodeheffer, 1976; Powell, Brasel, & Blizzard, 1967a, 1967b).

Morse, Sahler, and Friedman (1970) found that 29 percent of the abused children they studied were considered mentally retarded and 28 percent were significantly emotionally disturbed. These researchers concluded that family disorganization, poverty, minimal cognitive stimulation, and lack of love are known to impede emotional, neurological, and intellectual development in growing children. Others (Abram & Kaslow, 1976; Baron, Byar, & Sheaff, 1970; Martin, 1976) have shown that environmental factors may not only result in impaired thinking but may also be the basis for learning disabilities, tremors, uncoordination, impaired perception, impaired balance, and delayed language abilities.

Elmer (1967) found that abused children evidenced poor impulse control, poor self-concept, and frequent anger. In this study, anger was the most differentiating characteristic of physically abused children, and those abused children who remained in their environment had more severe emotional problems than those who had been removed from the home.

Overt and fantasy aggression in physically abused children who had been placed in foster homes was also studied by Rolston (1971). It was found that these children evidenced significantly less overt and fantasy aggression. They scored lower on truancy, quarrelsomeness, and destructiveness. These children were characterized by their docility, somberness, compliancy, noncompetitiveness, and eagerness to please others. They did, however, engage in more self-stimulatory activities, such as thumbsucking and masturbation. Fantasy aggression was seen in children who were abused before the age of three and who had a history of prolonged severe abuse rather than a series of isolated incidents.

There is an overwhelming amount of research on emotional problems associated with physical abuse. Bakan (1971) found that abused children developed traits that made them difficult to like, which invited further mistreatment. He cited such traits as fear of being alone, continual whining, shyness, depression, fear of new situations, hypersensitivity to pain, overreaction to hostility, hyperactivity, destructiveness, inability to help themselves, and turning their anger inward and blaming themselves.

Often emotionally disturbed children are products of atmospheres that are insensitive, imposing, punishing, and abusing. Monane, Leichter, and Lewis (1984) studied psychiatrically hospitalized children and adolescents and found a 42 percent prevalence of physical abuse in their histories. They concluded that the abused patients were similar symptomatically and diagnostically to the nonabused group so that emotional disturbance in the child, in and of itself, did not therefore account for their having been abused. Their abused subjects manifested much more violent behavior than the nonabused subjects. This finding lead Monane and his colleagues to believe that the youngsters' violence, rather than inviting parental attack, was a reaction to the way he or she had been treated and the violence that had been witnessed in the family. In 1979 Morgan studied the differences between abused emotionally disturbed and nonabused emotionally disturbed children assigned to special education classrooms in public schools and found mixed results in their behavior. Some of the abused subjects were more withdrawn, but would tantalize others into misbehavior, and some were more decidedly aggressive. Abused subjects in this study demonstrated more impulsivity, anger, and aggression; however, the abused subjects' acting-out behaviors were primarily yelling, making loud noises, sulking, making angry faces, and obscene gestures. These behaviors were followed almost immediately with overtures to make amends, in very disingenuous ways, with the teacher. In terms of their social behavior, the abused subjects' positive responses to their classroom teachers' authority did not transfer to other adults in the school. They were very reluctant to try different activities and displayed an exaggerated fear of failure by trembling and crying when confronted with a new lesson, activity, or situation. They often did not fight but provoked and encouraged other children to fight with each other. Their own aggression took the form of teasing and tormenting others with rude remarks but would quickly retract their behavior by telling their peers, "I was only kidding." They were as disingenuous with their peers as they were with their teachers. However, like the subjects in Monane, Leichter, and Lewis's (1984) study, Morgan's abused subjects were also similar symptomatically and diagnostically to the nonabused subjects. Therefore, the notion that children become emotionally handicapped because they have been abused could be strengthened by the similarities in these two studies. One major difference between these studies is that the subjects in one study (Monane et al., 1984) were hospitalized and the subjects in the other study (Morgan, 1979) were in public school special classes. It is impossible to know if the youngsters in one study were more severely disturbed than the youngsters in the other study. While hospitalization is not a certain criteria indicating degree and severity of emotional disturbance, the two different types of placements raise the possibility that the populations were not the same at all. It may be that the hospitalized subjects were indeed more severely disturbed and their problems were due to abuse, while the special class subjects were less disturbed and were abused because of their behavior and characteristics. This is one difference still leaves the question of cause and effect obscured.

Although done some years ago, a study by De Francis (1969) is still one of the most respected investigations conducted on the emotional effects of child sexual abuse. De Francis studied child victims of incest, rape, sodomy, and other forms of child molestation. In this study two-thirds of the children were evaluated to be emotionally disturbed by the offense and its consequences, and nearly one-fourth of the disturbed children had suffered severe, acute damage to their mental health. Some of the reactions shown by these children were anxiety, guilt, hostile aggressiveness, delinquency, antisocial adjustment problems, damage to their self-esteem, and repetitive imitative behavior of the sexual attack. De Francis also reported that the victims of incest are especially vulnerable and the guilt is often too enormous for the ego to accommodate, causing serious emotional damage, sometimes to the point of schizophrenia. Gordy (1983) found that grown women who had been sexually abused as children, abuse themselves with alcohol, drugs, or anorexia nervosa.

It has been shown that the combined effects of all the problems involved in incest cause, in some children, reactions close to psychotic states, such as prolonged confusional periods and rage reactions. A great variety of physical and emotional symptoms may occur following sexual assaults, which include enuresis, fears, hyperactivity, altered sleep patterns, phobias, compulsive play, learning problems, compulsive masturbation, depression, and anxiety (Adams-Tucker, 1982; Giarretto, 1976, 1982; Morgan, 1984; Schecter & Roberge, 1976; Schultz & Jones, 1983; Tilelli, 1980).

Although children of attacks by a stranger do not, in general, react as severely as when attacked by a father or father substitute, they do develop problems following such incidents. Typically, they develop eating and sleeping problems; negative feelings toward men they know as well as men they do not know; fearful of leaving their houses; some drop out of school entirely; and also manifest symptoms of withdrawal, confusion, anxiety, and guilt (Cohen, 1983; Peters, 1976; Shamray, 1980; Summit & Kryso, 1978; Woodling, 1981).

Prior to sexual abuse, only a few of the victims had displayed such behavior patterns as problems in school, running away, truancy, or drug and alcohol abuse. Most of the children got along well with friends at school and in their home communities. In other words, before a sexual-abuse experience, the victims were apparently well-adjusted, normal children (Adams-Tucker, 1982; Oliver, 1967; Schultz & Jones, 1983; Shah, 1982; Tilelli, 1980; Woodling, 1981).

One of the major findings in a study by Peters (1976) was that the sexual abuse of children involves little physical force. The lack of physical force was because 80 percent of the attackers were familiar power figures to the child: grandfather, father, uncle, babysitter, or friend of the family. This, in itself, may be a principal component in explaining why childhood sexual abuse is often the basis of psychiatric problems later in life.

Because many handicapped children cannot talk or do not realize there was any wrong-doing (e.g., the severely mentally retarded), we really have no idea of how many handicapped children have suffered from sexual abuse. One thing that has always been a concern of parents and teachers of mentally retarded children is their susceptibility to manipulation, extortion, and exploitation.

ABUSED BECAUSE THEY ARE HANDICAPPED

There are a number of studies demonstrating that abuse comes after the development of a handicapping condition. Premature infants are abused and neglected significantly more than the total population of infants. Apparently, the cause is related to the physical characteristics of the premature infant. These babies create negative or hostile reactions in the parents because they are small, unattractive, developmentally retarded, require special care, and have arrythmic, high-pitched cries (Frodi, 1981; Herrenkohl & Herrenkohl, 1979). It has been suggested that their crying is the final straw that triggers an abusive attack. Frodi (1981) reports that the majority of abusive mothers she interviewed mentioned "incessant crying," "grating sound of the cry," or "whining for prolonged periods of time." She continues by noting that,

> infant cries typically elicit two types of response propensities in adults: a tendency to intervene out of empathy and a tendency to intervene in an attempt to terminate a signal that is perceived as aversive. The probability of aggressive behavior is enhanced when aroused individuals are exposed to an aversive stimulus. The child may thereafter be perceived as aversive . . . even after the initial aversive features have been outgrown (p. 343).

Several studies examined cases where there were pre-existing handicapping conditions that provoked abuse because this type of child was unwanted or difficult to care for (Herrenkohl & Herrenkohl, 1979; Herrenkohl, Herrenkohl, & Egolf, 1983; Milner & Wimberley, 1980; Trout, 1983). Children with birth defects and physical problems were found to be significantly more likely to be targets for gross, life-threatening neglect. Mothers of cerebral-palsied infants were found to be highly negative and controlling, engaged in less smiling, less positive talking, and less physical closeness. The infants who were ill or handicapped and were physically abused developed personality problems and suffered from developmental delay at a rate that greatly exceeded what would be expected for the illness or handicap (Tyler & Kogan, 1977).

Another group of children with a handicapping condition that seems to make them particularly vulnerable to physical and emotional abuse is the emotionally disturbed youngster. These children were described by their mothers as having such problems as excessive eating or refusal to eat, eating inedible materials, temper tantrums, moodiness, sleep disorders, aggressiveness, running away, coming home late, lying, stealing, leaving without permission, and other unspecified behavior problems. Often they were described with such derogatory terms as bad, thick-headed, big mouth, two-faced, crabby, and clumsy. These children were found to be in significantly greater danger for being abused (Herrenkohl & Herrenkohl, 1979; Herrenkohl, et al., 1983; Milner & Wimberley, 1980).

AN OLD ISSUE WITH SOME NEW TWISTS

The abuse of handicapped children in residential and institutional settings is an old problem that is still with us. It is usually done knowingly by untrained or poorly trained nurses' aides, orderlies, hospital and institutional guards, and custodial staff. More recently, however, we are learning that professionals who are supposed to be trained to provide services to the handicapped can also become involved in abuse of these children, sometimes knowingly and sometimes unwittingly. Anyone with a predilection toward being abusive can, and some do, become abusive with handicapped youngsters under the guise that they are using highly specialized techniques, some of which are so barbaric that no knowledgable, ethical professional would ever claim that these are legitimate "techniques." These abusive "professionals" can get away with it, also, because they quote and cite literature to innocent, uneducated people (parents, student trainees, observers) that substantiates the type of treatment they perpetrate on their students and clients. In addition, many of the children and adolescents are so severely handicapped that they are unable or do not even know how to complain and speak-out for themselves (Institutional Child Abuse, 1977; Rothstein, 1985; Sluyter & Cleland, 1979).

The author personally heard an individual with a doctoral degree, referring to the severely and profoundly retarded, state that, "when they act like animals, you treat them like animals, and when they act like human beings then you treat them like human beings." Some of us still have a great deal of growing to do.

In 1976 Morgan noted that there is a higher incidence of all types of handicapped children who are abused and they comprise, to an ample degree, the special education clientele. We do know that the handicapped are at high risk for all forms of abuse, but quite often we do not have the exact means for identifying those who are being abused. For example, a great number of children who are severely mentally retarded are self-abusive and inflict their own wounds; but, are some of these children also being abused by others? In some cases they are, but it is very difficult, and in many instances impossible, to tell which wounds were the result of self-abuse and which wounds were inflicted upon the child by someone else. Many of these children are unable to speak, due to their limited intellectual abilities and lack of language development, and the professional learns next to nothing when asking them to tell what happened.

In matters pertaining to sexual abuse, again their limited abilities preclude the use of all the usual methods for gathering information (e.g., anatomically correct dolls, puppets, and interviewing). To add to the difficulty of identifying those handicapped children who need protection from abuse is the fact that some do not even realize they are being abused. This is especially true for those who are molested and sexually assaulted (Watson, 1984).

Finally, consider what would happen if these children could talk about their abuse. Would they be considered reliable and competent witnesses for their own defense? The question is rhetorical, and the answer is: Of course not! All an attorney has to do is bring forth the certified, diagnostic label of the child who has accused someone of abuse. Imagine the reaction when judge and jury hears that the child is mentally retarded, learning disabled, or emotionally disturbed. Imagine the reaction when expert witnesses are called and they detail the characteristics of children with the handicapping conditions of mental retardation, learning disabilities, or emotional disturbance. Most district attorneys would not touch such a case. Most justices would rule the child's testimony as incompetent and therefore inadmissable evidence. And last, if the case gets this far, most juries would be in such a confused state, filled with so much doubt, that such cases would rarely result in a favorable decision for the child.

To illustrate what is being described, following is an example of an interview between a social worker and a severely mentally retarded child. Someone reported that they had observed the abuse of children in a private clinic for the severely and profoundly retarded. While the author was not a personal witness to the following interaction, the event was described later by an individual directly involved. Therefore, while the dialogue is reconstructed to maintain privacy and protect the innocent, it is not fabricated.

SOCIAL WORKER: I see those sores on your arm. How did that happen?

CHILD: Cookie?

SOCIAL WORKER: No, I don't have a cookie. I have some candy mints. You can have one after we talk. Okay? How did you get those sores on your arms?

CHILD: Candy! [*screams unintelligible sounds*]. Candy?

SOCIAL WORKER: Okay, one candy—then talk. Understand? I want to know how you got those marks on your arms. Did someone do that to you?

CHILD: [*Now the child is chewing the candy and rocking in the chair. Leans over and bangs head on the table a couple of times.*] More cookie! Go store. Wash. [*Child shrieks, laughs, and stares off into space. Does not make eye contact with the social worker*]

SOCIAL WORKER: No more candy until we talk. I won't hurt you. I just want you to tell me how you got those marks—sores—hurts—boo-boos. See right here on your arms. Here and here and here. How did this happen?

CHILD: [*Laughs, rocks in chair. Begins to wave fingers in front of eyes.*] Candy! Cookie? [*Shrieks more unintelligible sounds. Slides out of chair to the floor and begins banging head on floor.*] Wash dish. Clean. [*More shrieking.*]

The social worker gives-up because obviously this child is not capable of relating to another person well enough to articulate anything that makes sense.

This illustration was used as an obvious example of why it is so difficult to precisely establish the number of handicapped chil-

dren who are being abused, cannot tell us about it and, consequently, cannot receive protection. It also demonstrates the
enormous problem we face in trying to determine if this type of
child has injuries that are totally self-inflicted, injuries sustained at
the hands of someone else, or a combination of both. The question still remains: Are many of these handicapping conditions the
result of abuse and neglect, or are handicapped children more vulnerable to being abused and neglected?

CHAPTER 4

People Who Abuse Children

The first question usually asked about parents who mistreat their children is, "How can people abuse children?" Phrased that way, the question is unanswerable. Attention has to be focused on the situations and characteristics of adults who are typically involved in the abuse of children. As in all types of abuse, these parents come from all the different racial, religious, economic, and ethnic groups; many have been abused children themselves. The only thing that can be said with any certainty about abusive parents is that they are people who struggle with a combination of factors and feelings that they experience as overwhelmingly stressful and for which they do not have coping skills.

Frequently, abusive parents find themselves in isolation; they do not have other adults (family or friends) providing them with emotional support. Generally they are people with low self-esteem, not liking themselves or knowing how to fulfill their own emotional needs. In many cases, although not all, higher rates of abuse are associated with undesirable economic conditions (Frodi, 1981; Garbarino & Ebata, 1983; Giovannoni, 1971; National Committee for Prevention of Child Abuse, 1983; Otto, 1984; Steinberg, Catalano, & Dooley, 1982).

Most reviews and studies of child-abusive parents reveal that it is not uncommon to find that these parents suffer from different mental retardation syndromes, drug and alcohol abuse, health problems, and various kinds of psychopathology, such as severe personality disorders, depression, and sadistic psychosis. They often appear beset with anxiety, hostility, and depression, making their responses to ordinary events inappropriate, impulsive, and excessive (Famularo, Stone, Barnum, & Wharton, 1986; Wolfe, 1984). Adequate social adjustment appears to be rare in these parents. More than half of abusive parents lack self-confidence and more than a third seem to be irresponsible and unreliable. It is also noted that parents who are not directly involved in inflicting injuries are passive, aversive, lacking in prosocial behaviors, and ineffective in protecting their children. This does not excuse them from responsibility and blame. By not stopping the abuse, they are equally culpable in a moral and ethical sense and in some cases both parents have been judged legally responsible (Johnson & Morse, 1968; Wolfe, 1984).

According to some researchers there are certain stresses both within and outside the home that can cause some parents, who ordinarily would not be abusive, to become so. Factors that have turned normally nonabusive people into abusive parents include: pregnancy forcing a marriage, an illegitimate child, a handicapping condition in the child that causes unacceptable behavior the parent views as deliberate, some type of interruption in the mothering process, marital and interfamily conflict, cultures that accept violence as a means of socialization, and a belief in corporal punishment (Delsordo, 1974; Garbarino & Ebata, 1983; James, 1975; Welsh, 1976b).

Although there are similarities among these parents, it is important that we do not try to stereotype child abusers; they are quite diverse in their backgrounds and characteristics. Professionals who come in frequent contact with parents notice that there are those who have some of the same backgrounds and characteristics as child abusers, but it cannot be concluded that they are abusers based on that information alone; that is stereotyping with the gravest consequences. There are differences in parents who perpetrate different kinds of abuse, but as described in the next section, there are some areas of overlap as well.

THE EMOTIONALLY ABUSIVE PARENT

According to the available information, consistent and extreme abusive behavior creates the greatest cause for concern. Isolated traumas apparently are not as damaging as constant and pervasive patterns of emotional neglect and emotional abuse (Garbarino & Garbarino, 1984). Some parents have unrealistic ideas about the needs of children and they do not understand how to care for them. Emotionally abusive parents, most commonly, are those who feel unable to resolve their own stress and control their own lives; the child becomes the target for mistreatment when they are unable to cope (Burgess & Conger, 1978; Garbarino & Garbarino, 1984; Garbarino & Gilliam, 1980; Gil, 1971; Justice & Justice, 1976).

In an article from the field of social work (Junewicz, 1983), emotional mistreatment of children is divided into two parts: emotional neglect, defined as parental omission in the child's care by providing no stimulation; and emotional abuse, defined as parental acts toward children that over-stimulate, such as verbal rejection and fear-inducing language or behavior. This article presents the results of a study conducted over a 3-year period that discusses 5 different family environments that produced emotional neglect and emotional abuse: (1) mental illness; (2) abuse of drugs and alcohol; (3) serious stress in relationships; (4) inadequate adjustment to life; and (5) serious personal conflicts. One hundred children from such family environments were studied and the majority of these children were found to be either emotionally neglected or emotionally abused. The family environments that seemed to produce the most emotional abuse were serious stress in relationships, and serious personal conflicts. The other three family environments split almost evenly between emotional abuse and emotional neglect with the exception of abusing drugs and alcohol, in which the majority of the children were judged to be predominantly emotionally neglected.

With the exception of Dean (1979) and Bowlby (1984), who describe situations in which the child is punished for normal activities, the literature on emotionally abusive behavior tends to focus primarily on what parents fail to do more than what they actually do to their children. Typically, emotionally abusive parents do not provide consistent love, acceptance, and praise that tells their children of their own self-worth. There is a notable lack of affection, continuity of care, guidance concerning behavior, and opportunities and approval for learning and growth. In addition, emotionally abused children are not allowed to become independent beings or engage in relationships that do not involve the family. Generally the parents fail to provide an adequate standard of reality or feelings of security. The parent–child relationship is, for the most part, cold and rejecting (Bowlby, 1984; Burgess & Conger, 1978; Garbarino & Garbarino, 1984; Rohner, 1975; Steele & Pollock, 1974; Whiting, 1978).

Rejection is a major theme that runs throughout the literature on emotional abuse; it is a prerequisite to emotional abuse, but abuse may not always be the outcome of rejection. It is important that this type of mistreatment is divided into abuse and neglect. At the very least it can be said, with some degree of certainty, that rejection of a child will lead to emotional neglect.

Rejection of handicapped children is often a typical reaction seen in many parents. It is not uncommon, even natural to an extent, to reject behavior that is unacceptable and displeasing; it becomes a problem when the parents reject the source of the behavior—their child. In most cases rejection is viewed as a defense mechanism in which the parents have persistent, unrealistic, negative values of the child. Rejection can be so subtle, that at times, it actually looks like acceptance. There are at least four ways that rejection of handicapped children can be manifested:

STRONG UNDEREXPECTATIONS OF ACHIEVEMENT. The parents devalue the child's abilities; when they set goals, they set them too low. The child becomes aware, at some level, of the parents' attitudes, begins to believe them, and behaves accordingly—creating a self-fulfilling prophecy.

SETTING UNREALISTIC GOALS. In this case the parents set goals that are too high. When the child cannot live up to these established goals and fails, then the parents feel justified in their negative attitudes toward the child.

ESCAPE. The most obvious form of escape is desertion of the child. Parents can engage in more subtle forms of escape that may not even be at a conscious level. They will find ways to be away from the child as much as possible during waking hours. For instance, they may take jobs that require extensive travel or late working hours; they may take frequent weekend trips; they may join social or charitable groups and those activities engage most of their time; and they may place their child in a distant residential facility when there are comparable facilities nearby.

REACTION FORMATION. This presents to the public the opposite of what the parents really feel—in an exaggerated way; e.g., they may buy every conceivable material object the child could need or want, so that on the surface it looks like they are indulging the child; but the real feelings of love and acceptance are missing (Colley, 1978; Evoy, 1983).

Evoy (1983) says that rejection is a reported subjective experience. He describes his clients' experience as, " . . . emotionally toned knowledge that they were not loved and wanted for themselves by one or both parents" (p. 14). We have not learned yet if a child will be or feel emotionally neglected if one parent rejects the child, but the other parent is accepting and loving. Evoy tells us that his patients sensed varying degrees of rejection that ranged from knowing they were hated and thought worthless, to feeling that their parents thought they loved them, or the parents wished they could love them, but were simply unable. Evoy noted that others have tried to put rejection on a scale ranging from "benign" to "malignant," but he does not believe there is "any substantial difference of hurtful experiential and/or behavioral characteristics in the rejected that appeared to be directly associated with their perceptions of different degrees of rejection by their parents" (p. 15). The major problems of Evoy's rejected patients were: damaged self-esteem, fear, guilt, depression, anger, hostility, and aggression.

We all realize how important parental acceptance is, but we do not have a good understanding of just how much rejection, by one or both parents, will affect a child most significantly. We assume, probably rightly so, that the effects are drastic. A parent cannot, of course, be taken to court for emotionally rejecting a child. Nothing could be accomplished by legal action if the child is not obviously and overtly abused; the courts cannot stop parents from feeling rejection toward their child. More importantly, the courts cannot make parents love their children!

Obviously, legal action is not possible or even desirable unless the outcome was that parents could be counseled and educated in parenting to the point of increasing more positive attitudes toward their children. Some parents might welcome the help when they realize they have not recognized at a conscious level how they actually feel about their child or why. It now seems that Dean's (1979) approach of identifying concrete behavior is the only realistic way to handle emotional abuse.

THE PHYSICALLY ABUSIVE PARENT

Elmer (1967) found that abusive mothers are less able to control themselves and their households. They experience more negative feelings towards their children and home lives. It was further noted that these families do not know who to rely on, and live under constant stress of a kind and degree unknown to those who are nonabusive. An extensive study of Black families who abuse their children found that these parents suffer from poverty, social isolation, and stressful relationships between themselves and with other family members (Daniel, Hampton, & Newberger, 1983; Garbarino & Ebata, 1983).

Abuse does not always begin at birth (Bowlby, 1984). Some parents have children so that they can feel needed. An infant is in constant need and so fulfills the parent's need to be needed. A critical stage in the parent–child relationship begins when the infant starts to show signs of independence, such as walking, playing with others, and then wandering greater distances from the parent. It is at this point in the child's life that love and trust are actually learned, but when a parent who needs to be needed can become abusive. The main caretaker, which is usually the mother, can react to this new independence in at least two adverse ways: restricting the child's development and causing extreme dependence, or rejecting the child and causing a disruption in the development of a sense of trust and self-worth (Brunnquell, Crichton, & Egeland, 1981).

Many parents experienced deprivation and abuse themselves as children, which created a tremendous need to feel needed. As adults, they hoped to find a human being to fill the emptiness they have felt since their childhood and hoped that a child of their own would fill that need. Abusive parents seem to have a pervasive feeling of never having been taken care of and consequently feel lonely, depressed, and anxious. Characteristically, they have low self-esteem and feel inferior, which makes them jealous and suspicious of even their own children. Out of their needs they feel their children should be capable of adult behavior and expect them to obey immediately, perform adult activities, and recognize and respond to every need of the parent. This seems to be a dominant theme among adolescent mothers and especially those who are themselves afflicted with some type of handicapping condition (Bowlby, 1984; Court, 1974; Davoren, 1974).

Whether realistic or not, many abusive parents view their children as abnormal in some way or another. As previously discussed, some abused children do have handicapping conditions that make them the target of parental attacks. In other cases, however, there are parents who just see their children as bad, or as a competitor or burden that must be obliterated, or, at the very least, made to suffer (Brunnquell et al., 1981; Delsordo, 1974; Gil, 1969; Ounsted et al., 1974; Soeffing, 1975).

Spinetta and Rigler (1972) discuss in great detail the personality characteristics of the abusive parent. According to these investigators they are classified into four groups: (1) those with constant and pervasive hostility and uncontrolled aggression; (2) those who are self-indulgent, rigid, compulsive, lack warmth, and blame their children for their problems; (3) those who are extremely dependent, passive, immature, depressed, unresponsive, moody, and compete with the child for the love and attention of the spouse; and (4) fathers who are unable to support their families and stay home while their wives work. Apparently these fathers are frustrated, threatened by the role reversal, and turn aggressively on their children.

Mahler's (1968) work on separation–individuation is of interest in the causal relationship of the abusive parent and aggression. According to Mahler, the child develops first in a phase of symbiosis with the mother. During this phase, the child behaves and functions as though the two are an indistinguishable system. The child learns to depend on the mother and experiences her as a love object. Martin and Rodeheffer (1976) state that abusive parents, having a distorted object-relationship themselves, are not able to tolerate the separation–individuation process in their children. Mahler concludes that when this process is impeded for whatever reason, there is a surplus of unneutralized aggression.

Masterson (1976) develops this concept of separation and individuation in his theory about the borderline psychotic adult. He states that the mother's own borderline syndrome is projected upon the child, making the youngster a nonperson. Children react by ignoring their own potentials in order to retain approval from their mothers. This type of relationship creates conflict and produces fears of abandonment. Abandonment conjures up a variety of feelings: fear, anger, guilt, depression, helplessness, and emptiness, which are all manifested in different degrees as the child goes through normal developmental traumas. The abandonment feeling is an internal experience for which the actual separation is only a precipitating influence. The depression involved may have the motivational power of suicidal despair.

Lystad (1975) notes that there is research that shows a relationship of infanticide to subsequent attempts or actual suicides of parents. She states that this may be the result of a fusion of identities between the mother and infant that took place during a postpartum depression. Masterson (1976) believes that borderline adults re-experience the anger and rage felt toward their own mothers when they were children and then project those feelings from the past onto their own children in contemporary situations. Depression and fear of separation can dominate this adult and make them susceptible to rage reactions. They frequently use the threat of abandonment as a disciplinary technique, which enforces compliance from the child but also creates fear. When children reach the stage where they feel a need to become individuals, and this is met with disapproval and withdrawal from a most significant person, then strong feelings of guilt and fear develop. When these children reach adulthood, to suppress the guilt and fear, they then resort to becoming clinging and dependent, which leaves them open to overwhelming feelings of helplessness and rage and causes them to become abusive themselves. Ideally what is needed, of course, is the means to identify those who are at risk for abusing their children and provide intervention to parents before the abuse occurs (McMurtry, 1985).

PERPETRATORS OF SEXUAL ABUSE

While this section will focus primarily on the parent, it is important for the reader to recognize other types of child molesters both within and outside of the family. Basically, child molesters fall into two categories: (1) family members who may be either homosexual or heterosexual (incest); and (2) pedophiles, a term reserved for strangers who can be either heterosexual or homosexual, and are prosecuted according to established laws for the crimes of rape or indecent behavior with a child. There are also accounts of children (nonfamily members) who sexually attack other children. Not all are cases of adolescents preying on smaller, weaker children; they include young children, who happen to be stronger and more aggressive, attacking other children who are their own age, younger, or even older than they. In one study, De Jong (1982) found that 10 percent of the 416 children admitted to an emergency room for sexual abuse had been attacked by assailants 10 years of age or younger.

The Sexually Abusive Parent

Incest has recently become a widely studied area of research with many questions about the causes and effects on the whole family. It cannot be viewed solely from an offender-victim stance. Usually, the entire family is involved in some way in its continuity and is affected by it (Cohen, 1983; Maisch, 1972; Oliver, 1967).

Most investigators report that brother-sister incest is the most frequent type, although rarely reported. Mother-son incest is thought to be very rare. Father-daughter and stepfather-daughter incest are the most prevalent forms of reported incest, the latter reported more frequently than any other type (Anderson & Shafer, 1979; Cohen, 1983; Giarretto, 1976; Kaufman, Peck, & Tagiuri, 1954; Machotka, Pittman, & Flomenhaft, 1967; Walters, 1975; Williams, 1981; Woodling, 1981). It may well be that father-daughter incest is just as prevalent as stepfather incest, if not more so, but perhaps wives are more willing to report stepfathers than biological fathers.

The cause of incest is clearly seen as a manifestation of a disturbance within the family, and when it occurs between father and daughter, it develops most often within a background of disharmony and disorganization. Most investigators note that incest occurs predominantly in homes where there is lower social prestige, but on the average, the family lives comfortably in a financial sense. Incestuous relationships do not appear to be episodic but are more drawn-out, lasting at least a year and usually more. Despite the fact that some of these relationships can go on for many years, rarely is it the mother who reports the offense. In most cases, authorities find out through some outside source (Cohen, 1983).

It appears that there is a complicated interpersonal triangle, in which contributions are made by the nonactive members. From available research (Anderson & Shafer, 1979; Cohen, 1983; Gordy, 1983; Machotka et al., 1967; Maisch, 1972), the components that create a climate for incest consist of:

1. The incest usually begins following sexual estrangement between husband and wife, most frequently occurring because of some real or perceived loss of the wife; e.g., through death, divorce, separation, mental or physical illness, marital strife, or a new job that takes the mother out of the home for extended periods.

2. Generally, the wife is extremely dependent, immature, and feels inadequate as a mother and a woman, which causes her to reverse roles with her daughter and push the child

into adult responsibilities. Collusion by the mother is made possible through very strong denial of the incestuous relationship, and some mothers have been known to directly encourage father–daughter intimacy.

3. Frequently, the daughters see their mothers as cruel and rejecting, making the relationship with the father extremely important in the sense of taking revenge on the mother, and also receiving some of the affection and attention denied by her. Also, when the mother is emotionally unavailable because of mental illness, and the father is the only source of affection, a climate for incest develops.

Fathers involved in incest have been found to range from mentally average men who adequately take care of their families, to those who have problems with alcoholism and little self-control. Incestuous fathers range from psychologically normal to abnormal, with no consistent personality patterns dominating. Overall, however, they do have some characteristics that reappear in many studies: (1) they try to control the lives of all the family members by whatever means possible; (2) they try to justify and rationalize the incest by claiming to be protecting their daughters from outside influences and teaching them the "facts of life"; (3) their needs for attention and affection cannot be met through nonphysical or nonsexual means; and (4) they are considered emotionally immature (Anderson & Shafer, 1979; Gordy, 1983; Machotka et al., 1967).

With the exception of mothers who are definitely mentally ill and do not or cannot stop the incest, most mothers have been described as normally intelligent and not appearing psychologically unfit in any observable way. In general, they have been described as weak, submissive, depressed, and occasionally promiscuous. Some have come from deprived backgrounds in which they had been deserted by their own parents. Generally, they give up their role as wife and mother and turn this over to their daughters, including the sexual role, in an attempt to be nurtured as if they were the child. Many had incestuous pasts as well, and are unable to avoid or terminate relationships in which they are mistreated. They may have sexual problems, such as sexual dysfunction, or they may have latent lesbian tendencies and, in some cases, do seek-out lesbian relationships (Anderson & Shafer, 1979; Cohen, 1983).

The Stranger—Pedophiles

Pedophilic offenses fall into two cateogires: heterosexual and homosexual. Heterosexual pedophilia is by far more common than homosexual pedophilia. The sexual activity is of an immature type, meaning that the behaviors are usually restricted to fondling, exhibiting, looking, and masturbation with no attempt at coitus. While the majority of sexual acts involving men and girls are of this type, there are pedophiles who do rape. In cases involving male homosexual pedophiles who attack boys, the sexual acts are usually more aberrant, aggressive, and brutal (Brant & Tisza, 1977; Ellerstein & Canavan, 1980).

The number of women sex offenders has always been thought to be extremely small (Kinsey, Martin, Pomeroy, & Gebhard, 1953). However, since there have been cases recently adjudicated that involved women teachers (primarily preschool), research in this area is presently being pursued quite vigorously. Even though the results are not available, rumor is that it is still a very rare phenomenon to encounter women pedophiles.

The pedophile has commonly been stereotyped as a "dirty old man," but the age distribution actually falls into three groups: (1) adolescents characterized by a lag in psychosexual maturation; (2) those in their mid-to-late 30s who experience a breakdown in their adjustment to the demands of the adult world in general, and family relationships in particular; and (3) lonely and impotent men in their late 50s to early 60s (Karpman, 1954; Peters, 1976; Tilelli, 1980; Woodling, 1981).

In terms of a psychiatric profile, child molesters are often diagnosed as psychopaths or sociopaths who are passive-aggressive and extremely immature, with strong feelings of inadequacy and insecurity. Pedophiles have been assessed with every conceivable psychological test and consistently show high levels of anxiety, dependency, and regressiveness. It also appears that they have considerable low self-esteem and are extremely lacking in sensitivity to the needs of others. A small percentage of pedophiles have been diagnosed as schizophrenic or paranoid (Abrahamsen, 1960; Ellerstein & Canavan, 1980; Oliver, 1967; Woodling, 1981).

Frequently, pedophiles are alcoholics who do not relate well to their adult peers and have poor relationships, if any, with adult women. Gigeroff (1968) found that 45 percent of the pedophiles he studied were alcoholics or very heavy drinkers, and that economic stress made them more prone to pedophilia, as well as a variety of other types of antisocial behavior.

Pedophiles seem to need some unusual or unique experience to stimulate their sexual drives. Whether heterosexual, homosexual, or bisexual, the majority of them are psychosexually infantile with a predilection for young children. They are very adept at attracting the attention of children and gaining their confidence and friendship, thus luring them into situations in which sexual abuse can occur. Because their own personal sense of inadequacy creates a fear of impotence after repeated unsatisfactory sexual relationships with adults, they turn to children (Ellis & Abarbanel, 1967; Karpman, 1954; Woodling, 1981).

As has been stated several times earlier, abused children frequently become abusive adults. This happens to be especially true of the adult pedophile. They come from predominately low socioeconomic areas, and as children were often neglected and abused, although not necessarily sexually abused (De Jong, 1982; Gigeroff, 1968).

A common finding is that pedophiles never had adequate or accurate sexual information during their developmental years but instead experienced continuous traumatic reactions to even normal sexual experiences. Normal childhood sexual experiments, such as masturbation, were treated as great offenses and typically they feared and received excessive punishment from the parents for such activities. A substantial proportion of the case histories of pedophiles reveals that they had experienced, in early childhood, incestual and homosexual attacks. Those who had been involved in homosexual incest had pronounced fears of impotence, sterility, and physical disfigurement (Adams-Tucker, 1982; De Jong, 1982; Oliver, 1967).

From the available information, most of these individuals have come from unstable homes in which they felt rejected by their mothers, and in which their fathers were characterized as alcoholic, cruel, and domineering. Their homes were dominated by stress and strife, with the parents in constant conflict with each other (Gigeroff, 1968; Woodling, 1981).

A checklist of the characteristics and behaviors of abusive parents can be found in Appendix A, Form 2.

CHAPTER 5

Emergent Problems
Related to Child Abuse

Child abuse is a broad topic that is currently receiving widespread attention. On almost a daily basis a child-abuse case of some type is in the news. Many such cases now involve the accusation of teachers—some of which are true and some that are not. In an earlier chapter the author mentioned that teachers have recognized that it is not only untrained support staff who abuse the handicapped: professionals with college degrees are also abusing children. Some abuse children unwittingly and some are deliberate. In this chapter an attempt will be made to at least discuss the issues and create some guidelines to protect the teacher from unintentionally abusing children, to protect children from abuse by others, and to protect the teacher from false accusations of child abuse. This chapter is not only about protecting innocent children—it is intended to help protect *all* the innocents.

ABUSE IN THE WORKPLACE

The issue of abusive people using abusive practices under the guise of "professional techniques" is presented in this section in an effort to help the teacher and prospective teacher avoid unintentional abuse of handicapped children. In the teaching, care, and treatment of handicapped children there are several technical terms that are part of the special education nomenclature, terms that are used to discuss what are supposed to be different methods for managing undesirable behaviors that some handicapped children manifest in great abundance. On the surface these terms would seem to be different approaches, and underneath they are supposed to be different. In many cases, however, they are not so different because they are being used by untrained, poorly trained, or ill-intentioned "professionals," as well as unknowledgable, innocent, gullible students. The terms that are indistinguishable, when used by the aforementioned people, include the broad categories of behavior modification, punishment, discipline, aversive conditioning, and corporal punishment. For instance, the technique of behavior modification emphasizes positive reinforcement for appropriate behavior, and punishes most often by removal of an opportunity to receive positive reinforcement. Aversive conditioning is only a small part of behavior modification; an example of aversive conditioning would be isolating an uncontrollable child. Discipline is the teaching of appropriate behavior by establishing rules the student must follow, or be excluded from school. Corporal punishment, of course, is bodily pain inflicted on the child. In the wrong hands, whichever term is used, they all amount to the same thing—*abuse!*

Some of the finest professionals and true experts in the behavior-modification field are at the Universities of Kansas, New Mexico, Virginia, and Washington. Other universities have experts in this field also, but the author has singled out those that have programs with which she is most familiar. If a teacher or student has doubts about the appropriate use of some of the procedures they have learned or are learning, one alternative would be to write to the professors at these universities. Being the kind of professionals they are, they usually are most willing to share what they know with someone who wants to learn. In the meantime there are also some excellent articles that should be consulted (e.g., Buddenhagen, 1971; Gardner, 1969; Nolley, Boelkins, Kocur, Moore, Goncalves, & Lewis, 1980; Roos, 1974; Wherry, 1983).

In Chapter 3, an interview was described that took place between a social worker and a severely mentally retarded child. The purpose of presenting that dialogue was to illustrate how difficult it is to verify if abuse has occurred and who perpetrated the abuse when asking this type of child to tell what he or she knows. With the intent of impressing upon the reader it is essential to learn how things can go awry, other events will be described that are related to this shocking case.

An individual in the community observed student teachers at a day-care center shouting at and slamming a large stick on nearby surfaces in front of severely mentally retarded students. The observer reported to Child Protective Services a belief that the handicapped students in the day-care center were being abused. When the student teachers were interviewed, they had been well-prepared for the social worker's questions by the "professional" in charge of the day-care center: They innocently and gullibly explained they were using behavior modification, specifically aversive conditioning. The shouting and stick-banging were intended to produce a "startle effect" that was designed to stop self-abusive and bad behavior. They were also instructed not to volunteer information that was not directly asked for by the investigator. The outcome of the interview between the social worker and one of the retarded youngsters has already been described.

Other incidents had happened in this day-care center that were never told to the social worker. An older, more mature student teacher revealed to another person that clients in the center were slapped, pinched, wrestled to the ground and "straightjacketed"—made to wear clothes in which they had urinated and soiled. For severe acting-out their pants were removed and they were made to sit in a bucket of ice. This was "aversive condition-ing" as described and taught by the "professional" in charge of the day-care center, but it is child abuse in its clearest form. The mature student who reported this to a trusted person, had had disagreements with the person in charge of the day-care center over the methods used with the handicapped and had been threat-ened with failing student teaching and not graduating, and thus did not report the abuse to the social worker.

The naive and gullible younger student teachers believed they were learning acceptable practices and techniques for working with this particular handicapped population. In their innocence they wrote about their experience of having been accused of child abuse and how people did not understand the complexity of working with such handicapped youngsters. Following are a few excerpts from the diary reports written by two of the student teachers:

STUDENT A: Other people are not aware of training techniques, such as behav-ior modification, which is often used when working with severe students. They would get upset because of the techniques we sometimes used to get the mentally retarded to behave. The whole incident upset and scared me so much that I don't think I want to work with the handicapped if this is the way it is going to be.

STUDENT B: To clear any misconceptions, the techniques which we employed were explained. Even after citing the research found in the special-education journals, people still did not really understand why we did the things we did. Later though, I began to question what I had been taught about working with the handicapped. Even after the charges had been dropped, I could not help but wonder if I had been cruel. Now that time has passed, I realize how poorly informed normal people are about special populations and that we all did what was best.

Several things are particularly sad about this incident. The stu-dent teachers were made to believe, by an authority figure they admired and trusted, that these are acceptable methods of treat-ment, and, to date, that is all they have learned. They were accused of abuse and treated with contempt for behaviors they thought were legitimate techniques, and they began to feel guilty. Since that was all they had learned, and the psychological guilt was difficult to bear, they started the mental process of justifying what happened by attempting to establish the ignorance of others. A potentially good special-education teacher had been driven from the field. Other students' sense of morality and ethical behavior were compromised by the threat of failing a requirement and not earning their college degrees. Finally, because the students had graduated and had learned only one approach, this treatment will be perpetuated and handicapped individuals will continue to be abused.

Where do people get such distorted and skewed ideas regarding treatment methods for the handicapped? They get them from poorly trained authority figures and from journals; if it is seen in writing in a journal, it must be true and right! For example, here are a few quotes from an article (Johnson, 1981) in which the author uses one of the most preposterous euphemisms ever concocted—"corporal communication." He begins his article by describing the population of handicapped children he is suggesting will benefit from corporal communication.

> Children who have very little language, children with limited sensory ability, children whose inner world is a poor map of the actual world of reality, children who have difficulty moving, children still in the Piagetian sensory-motor stage of development . . . (p. 352).

Elsewhere he says,

> There is literature in psychology which substantiates the common sense observation that physical discomfort can cause organisms to change their behavior. . . . Pain is [sic] appropriate amounts can teach some important dimensions of what it means to be human . . . (p. 353).

This attitude is presented again:

> . . . children experience some reasonable pain and discomfort in order to become more self-controlled and more human . . . (p. 356).

What is reasonable pain? Who decides how much pain is reasonable for another person? Unfortunately, child abusers know without reading psychology, that "physical discomfort" forces children to change their behavior. Clearly, the author does not consider these children human beings. How does one teach human beings to become human beings when they *are* human beings? Can other living nonhuman organisms be taught how to be a human? Are these ludicrous questions? Of course they are because the author of that article published in a professional journal made ludicrous statements. By their mere existence, these children are humans. What *is* needed is for more of us to be concerned with *our* being *humane*. Humane, according to Webster's Unabridged dictionary definition, is "characterized by tenderness and compassion for the suffering or distressed." This characteristic, this humaneness, is one of the special qualities that attract most of us to the field of special education where we can work with the handicapped to help alleviate some of their suffering and distress.

In another part of this same article the author draws the analogy that withholding doses of pain could be considered passive abuse because it would be like not taking your child to the dentist (where presumably he means the child gets a dose of intentional but needed pain) to correct a problem. The logic in this analogy contains a nearly laughable non sequitur. Obviously, dentists do not intentionally inflict pain to be successful in their work. In fact, these days they work with great effort to prevent pain and make the necessary corrections with as little discomfort to the patient as possible. If they accomplish painless dentistry, they consider themselves successful. Dentists do not set out deliberately with the idea that, "Now I am going to punish you with a small dose of pain to change what is wrong with your teeth." The author's analogy would almost be humorous if he was not serious and had not presented this in a professional journal, in which ideas to help better the lives of the handicapped are being shared with other professionals and students.

Why Johnson (1981) wishes to refer to the inflicting of pain as "corporal communication" will not be speculated upon. Others are more forthright in what they discuss: they do not attempt to speak with deceptive, affected elegance; inflicting pain is corporal *punishment* (MacMillan, Forness, & Turmbull, 1973; McDaniel, 1980; Piele, 1978; Propst & Nagle, 1981).

McDaniel (1980) clearly defines corporal punishment and warns teachers that, with increased instances of punishment, they might experience "increased instances of negligence cases brought against teachers. Finding alternatives to legally dangerous punishment practices is a high priority for educators" (p. 10). Special note of the definition of corporal punishment should be taken and, while reading the definition, a reflection on what took place in the day-care center incident. The definition according to McDaniel reads:

This is a form of corrective discipline that involves physical force and the inflicting of bodily pain on the student. Typically, corporal punishment practices include paddling (with or without an instrument), slapping, cracking hands with a ruler, pinching, pushing, hitting, hammerlocks and other wrestling holds, and exotic techniques such as finger holds ("milk the rat") and ear twists. In some cases, courts have extended the definition to include threatening gestures and psychologically damaging techniques of punishment that humiliate students or create mental anguish (p. 10).

Recalling the definition of emotional abuse, it included inflicting public humiliation and mental anguish. Paradoxically, emotional and physical abuse is illegal, but corporal punishment has been ruled by the Supreme Court as legal. In a great many cases, however, it is very difficult to distinguish child abuse from corporal punishment. Even more absurd and difficult to understand is why the law protects adult criminals in prison from corporal punishment but not children in public schools. An adult can pinch and hit and do all kinds of things to children, but if the same things were done to adult criminals it would be considered cruel and unusual punishment. Sooner or late this conflict of logic will have to be resolved in the United States. In Great Britain, the House of Commons has already passed a bill abolishing corporal punishment in public schools.

In a very interesting and timely article, Rothstein (1985) discusses professional misconduct of educators towards the handicapped and explains why misconduct, in most cases, should be subject to common-law tort action. Her description of "misconduct" is especially pertinent to us. The reader is encouraged to peruse this quite lengthy article. Below, are some of the statements most critical to teachers:

"Whether educational personnel are prepared or not, they may be held accountable for serious misconduct in educating handicapped children. This accountability may result in large damage rewards in some cases" (p. 351).

"When dealing with handicapped children, the relevant considerations should be not only age and maturity but also physical and mental capacity" (p. 370).

"Recovery under common law tort principles requires the following elements: 1. A duty to adhere to a particular standard of conduct or to exercise reasonable care. [*punctuation added*] 2. Breach of the duty or violation of a standard. [*punctuation added*] 3. Causal connection between the breach and injury. [*punctuation added*] 4. Resultant injury" (pp. 367–368).

Misconduct includes but is not limited to, " . . . failure to take adequate precautions in supervising certain types of potentially dangerous activities . . . " (p. 350).

" . . . the negligent or intentional infliction of emotional distress—humiliating a student unreasonably in front of classmates. . . ." (p. 350).

" . . . inappropriate behavior management . . . " (p. 350).

" . . . negligent programming—the use of an educational methodology that would be grossly inappropriate for the handicapped child" (p. 350).

"Common law tort principles generally provide for recovery for infliction of emotional distress where the 'conduct exceed(s) all bounds usually tolerated by decent society, of a nature which is especially calculated to cause, and does cause, mental distress of a very serious kind'" (p. 354–355).

" . . . there should be little difficulty in making a case for intentional infliction of emotional distress where a teacher or administrator or other school employee engaged in outrageous conduct towards a handicapped student which resulted in emotional distress" (p. 355).

" . . . a handicapped child is likely to be especially 'sensitive, susceptible and vulnerable' to severe emotional distress which may not usually be expected of the average child of the same age group" (p. 356).

"For example, tying a student into his chair because he constantly runs out of the room may result in severe emotional distress for a mentally retarded student who is unusually susceptible to emotional distress from this type of disciplinary measure" (p. 356).

" . . . for a handicapped child, . . . may result in severe emotional distress both from the emotional anxiety caused by the restraint and from the humiliation and embarrassment caused to most highly sensitive children" (p. 356).

Rothstein (1985) also gives other examples of actions that may be considered misconduct by teachers of handicapped youngsters; these are related primarily to negligence in supervision. There are many considerations in which teachers of the handicapped must be well informed; they need to understand the possible consequences of certain actions. It is a fact that a number of children with Down's Syndrome are afflicted with respiratory and cardiac weakness. Extreme fear produced by startling or threatening behavior could possibly cause cardiac failure. Other children with neurological disorders, who have implanted shunts, can suffer severe damage or death if they are shaken, slapped, or hit, and the shunt is dislodged or damaged.

REPORTING PROCEDURES

To avoid being unintentionally abusive, a teacher must be well-educated and knowledgable about the various handicapping conditions, and must also be thoroughly familiar with appropriate use of certain highly sophisticated techniques. If not, until more is learned, they should go by the old axiom, "if you can't help, at least don't hurt." In addition, teachers are culpable and could also be prosecuted if they fail to report known abuse of a child for which they have responsibility (their student), or cover-up for someone who is abusing a child (Kassel, 1985).

Talking To The Child And The Parent

It is not the job of the instructor to investigate or do detective work in the case of suspected child abuse. However, following are some examples of possible situations that could arise and how they might best be handled:

• The child comes to school with a serious injury.

> DO SAY: "Oh, that looks painful." How did that happen?" Or, "What happened?" Or, "Can you tell me where you got that burn, bruise, or bite?" Supposing the child replies, "Mommy burned me." You would want to follow-up with another question such as, "How did that happen?" Then the child says, "With the iron." You say, "Irons get very hot. How did it happen that you got burned with your mother's iron?" Notice you do not say why did your mother burn you or how did your mother burn you? Instead you say, "How did you get burned with your mother's iron?" There is the possibility that after asking the questions in this open, nonthreatening manner that a real abuse incident might be told to you in detail. But by asking just a few more open questions in the manner described, the burn incident could turn out to be an unfortunate accident that could happen in any household. For instance, after the question of, "How did it happen that you got burned with your mother's iron?", the child may tell you, "I wanted to iron too—my doll's clothes; Mommy said I can't play with the iron and grabbed it from me—I grabbed it back and got burned."

DO: Write this down in detail for your files; you are not ready to report child abuse unless the child comes to school with more injuries. Generally, school nurses will make a report after identifying more than two injuries.

DO NOT: Confront the child directly and sternly with a question like, "Did your mother burn you?" "Who did this terrible thing to you?" "Have they done that to you before?" Questions phrased this way are often interpreted by children as threatening. They detect some possible danger in telling the truth because of the urgency or concern expressed in your voice, as well as the accusatory tone that their parents are bad and therefore will be punished. Remember you are an authority figure to the child and if you can punish the children maybe you can punish the parents. They are most likely to lie and say that mom or dad didn't do it—brother or sister did. Or, they don't know how they got it; they can't remember.

- The parents of a child who shows signs and symptoms of abuse come for a school conference.

DO: Express your concern about the child's symptoms and signs you have noticed. For example, "Jill seems afraid of most people at school." "John sure has a lot of bumps and bruises." Listen carefully to what they say and how they explain their child's behavior or injuries. Observe their behavior. Write all of this down in detail after the conference and use the checklist for parents in Appendix A, Form 2.

DO NOT: Accuse them of child abuse, argue with them, or express disbelief in what they say; or tell them their child has accused them of abuse; or show them poor or failing work the child has done or discuss any of the child's misbehavior.

- You have filed a child-abuse report and the parents learn that you made the charges. They appear at your door (classroom or home) in an angry, ugly mood, perhaps shouting that you are a liar and asking why you reported them.

> DO: Remain calm and say only the following: "I am required by law to report any injury that is hard to explain in order to get help for you and the child." Hang up the phone. Close your door. If they are in your classroom, call the principal to remove them if they will not leave. Leave the rest up to the Child Protective Agency in charge.

> DO NOT: Lose your own control; threaten them with any type of repercussion; go into detail explaining every sign, symptom, and reason for filing a report; let them into your house; let them stay in your classroom; lie, saying you did not make the report; blame someone else; discuss it in the teachers' lounge; give interviews or turn over any of your written documentation to the news media.

- These parents will undoubtedly carry a grudge against you forever, so it is unlikely that you will ever work with them in parent conferences. If, however, after the matter has been resolved and they have been in or are in family therapy and express an interest in their child's improvement, you must work with them as professionally as possible. Give them the same courtesy and school information that you would any other parent. Make sure the child's next teacher has background information on the child and understands that the parents have or are trying to improve. It is possible that a new teacher will be able to establish a better working relationship with that parent. Remember that if they do, it is not because they are better teachers than you are or that you are not as good. Your relationship with the abusing parent was under very different circumstances. If the parents have been helped, they are very different people than when you had to teach their child and try to work with them. *You did the right thing and the best thing for the child!* It was your job responsibility and you fulfilled it admirably.

Writing The Report

Teachers can make an anonymous report, but it is better if they identify themselves. If a report is filed and if it is proven to be a mistake, teachers are granted immunity from civil or criminal action if they acted in good faith (National Committee for Prevention of Child Abuse, 1983). This good faith immunity protects both professional and nonprofessional persons. Teachers or other school personnel, however, should prepare well-documented reports, not because they are any less immune but because they are professionals and the protection of children is part of their professional responsibilities. The document should be given the same professional attention that is used when doing any other work-related material. The four forms in Appendix A are designed to assist the professional in keeping accurate data so that a well-documented report can be prepared. As will be seen in the section on false accusations, these forms can also help protect the professional from being accused.

Appendix B contains toll-free hot line numbers provided by AT&T. The professional should make a call when he or she has the data together and knows what to talk about when the investigating social worker comes to interview.

A follow-up letter, with a copy for the files, to the phone call is important to document that a report was filed in keeping with both teacher responsibilities and with the law. To keep good faith and maintain immunity, this letter should be very objective; it does not name-call. For example, the professional does not write in the letter that it is to inform the Agency that Mr. and Mrs. Doe are child abusers. Samples of how to prepare this most important report are seen in Appendix C.

FALSE ACCUSATIONS AGAINST TEACHERS

These are difficult times for teachers: there are accusations of teacher incompetence. Currently, there is forced competency testing of teachers in which failure could mean a lost job and the end of a career. There are all-encompassing criticisms of the public education system in which teachers are finding themselves in lead stories and front-page headlines in the news media. In general, they are being represented to the public in the most unflattering manner and, as a result, parents have become less trusting of the ability of teachers to meet the needs of their children.

There is now a strange and dangerous new phenomenon to add to the difficulties and torments of teachers—false accusations of all types of child abuse: physical, emotional *and* sexual. From the author's vantage point, those in the most jeopardy for accusations that could lead to criminal proceedings are preschool teachers and school counselors. This is true for preschool teachers because of the recent number of sexual-abuse cases involving preschools that have reached the courts and have received sensational media coverage. Parental and societal concern has now reached a fever pitch, and it is almost akin to the old witch hunts: Everyone is looking for it everywhere. Another reason that preschool teachers are vulnerable is because of the age of the child they work with and the types of activities that are common in the preschool curriculum (e.g., field trips away from the school). This will be dealt with in greater detail later. School counselors are vulnerable because they work with students in a very different capacity than other school personnel: they meet with students privately, behind closed doors, and with no witnesses to what really occurs in their offices.

As momentum builds, however, any teacher could be put in the position of having to defend him or herself against the false accusation of child abuse. Men are in a more precarious position, but women are no longer exempt from the same accusations (even in accusations of sexual abuse). What is behind this dreadful and disturbing trend?

Before discussing the most malicious reasons for people making false accusations, careful consideration must be taken, remembering that children are and have been abused by some caretakers who are supposed to be the most trusted individuals in society: priests, ministers, and teachers. It is common knowledge, for instance, that in high schools there have been teachers who have sexually molested their young students. We are all aware that we have undesirables in our profession, to the same extent and probably in the same proportion as other professions (Winks, 1982).

Because of the McMartin Preschool (Sheehy, 1984) tragedy in Manhattan Beach, California parents abruptly became aware that the most horrible things can happen to their children in the most unsuspected places by the most unsuspected people. Instances of the sexual abuse of young children made the national news again when preschool teachers and staff were arrested in Malden, Massachusetts and in the Bronx, New York. Many parents are now piqued and fearful, and the slightest out-of-the-ordinary incident involving their children will send some rushing with great urgency to investigate (*Harvard Law Review* Notes, 1985).

If incidents are handled properly there should be no unjust repercussions. It is positive, on one hand, to have parents more attentive to their children: it will help prevent child abuse. On the other hand, when people are ill-intentioned in their accusations, or when things are not handled properly, careers and lives are destroyed. Teachers are now in the peculiar position of trying to protect children from child abuse, and also trying to protect themselves from false accusations of child abuse.

Malicious Reasons For False Accusations

Following, are some true stories that will probably frighten many teachers and make them very anxious. Hopefully so, for it is the author's intention to jolt educators to attention; there are actions that educators will be told to take that they will not want to do; also, they will be told which actions not to take that some (even supervisors) will say must be done. Some of these actions are contrary to the author's natural inclinations and what has always been her approach to children. Most students, colleagues, and other practitioners would probably classify the author as a humanistically oriented educator, both in theory and practice, being a child advocate. The author is not prone to frivolity, and can, when necessary, be brutally practical. Professionals and educators must be able to be practical also, in order to avoid unnecessary painful experiences and protect themselves from unwarranted damage to their reputations and careers. Following are several reasons as to why false accusations might be brought against an educator:

1. Some parents see an opportunity for financial gain by bringing charges and a law suit against a person working in an organization that has insurance and will make large settlements.

2. There are parents who have been abusing their own children and when someone is about to turn them in, they instruct their children to accuse someone else. When very young children are involved, this can be easily accomplished.

3. Some prosecuting attorneys are intent upon building their own reputations and careers at other's expense. Winning a sensational case brings them great notoriety. Justice is *not* their priority.

4. Some parents "get it in" for a teacher and make an accusation that could end a career.

5. We have been told many times that children do not lie, especially about sexual abuse. That has been proven to be a myth (Howson, 1985). Some children do lie. Some children "get it in" for a teacher and make such accusations in order to get even. This happens primarily with older children who are savvy about sex. They have seen the TV shows, attended the sex-abuse educational programs, and have a good understanding of just how serious their accusations are and what it can mean to the teacher.

An example of the motive of financial gain as a reason for false accusation involved a case in which a teacher had been accused of sexually abusing more than one child in a preschool. The parent that first brought the charge against the teacher was in debt and out of work. The preschool's insurance company paid the parents a very sizable sum of money for damages.

An example of counter-abuse involved a 3-year-old child who was being sexually abused by the father. The grandparent was suspicious and threatened to go to the authorities. The preschool teacher was accused instead, and the charges were brought by the father. Couldn't the child tell the truth? In the mind of a 3-year-old, the truth *was* told. At this age, what the parent says *is* reality—it *is* truth!

An example of attorney manipulation involved an accusation of sexual abuse toward a teacher. Through a number of legal maneuverings the prosecuting attorney managed to have testimony withheld from the jury that could have cleared the defendant. The case was too sensational and important to the prosecutor's career to lose just for the sake of justice.

An example of parental revenge involves a parent who had a reputation for being at odds with the world. She consistently moved her child from one school to another, always claiming the teacher was no good. One teacher stood up to the woman and told her forthright that the child was spoiled and would not work and that was why she had not been achieving in school. The parent accused the teacher of physical and emotional abuse, and the child provided corroboration for ther mother's story.

An example of a child's false accusations involved a 12-year-old girl who was placed in a classroom for emotionally disturbed children. She missed her bus and asked the teacher for a ride home. The teacher gave her a ride home, and some time later the girl told a counselor that the teacher asked her to do "nasty things." The girl told others besides the counselor and each time she told the story, different aspects changed. Everyone was certain that the girl has lied because the teacher was strict and demanding. Although the teacher was not guilty of the accusation, she was never innocent—people still wondered about her. It damaged her reputation and she quit her teaching career to salvage her mental health.

Hidden Meanings And Misunderstandings

In this section a few examples of other ways in which false accusations can come about will be discussed:

1. A teacher in a center for the severely and profoundly handicapped changed the diapers on a child and was accused of sexual abuse for touching the genitalia, although it was for cleansing purposes and there were several witnesses to verify that proper care was being given. Rather than fight this through the courts and suffer a scandal, the center settled out of court and closed down. They considered the care of such children and the possibility of more misunderstandings, scandals, and law suits far too risky.

2. An 8-year-old girl of divorced parents lived with her mother, who was absorbed with her work and traveled a great amount of the time. The girl had weekend visiting privileges with her father. A friend of the girl had been involved in a sex-abuse case in which her father was accused; this resulted in her friend receiving a great deal of attention from her mother. The girl in this example copied her friend's story and accused her father of the same thing. This resulted in the child also receiving the attention she wanted from her mother, but she also became a very disturbed child when her father was sent to prison and she became aware of why he was there.

3. A 4-year-old child happened to tell his mother of "funny games" he played with the babysitter, Karen. Karen was a mentally retarded adolescent, and the daughter of the landlord. Somehow, in the emotional upheaval and confusion, the parent understood the child to say "Erin," the name of child's preschool teacher. The teacher is accused. In actuality, this is a case of a handicapped child perpetrating abuse.

4. A 3-year-old girl was, as her mother described, going through her "gross stage": she liked to get a mouth full of peanut butter and mushed-up bananas and open wide for all to see the contents. When her mom or dad tried to give her a hug and a kiss, she stuck out her tongue to slobber on their faces. When the maternal grandmother was babysitting, she got a slobbery tongue kiss, believed the child had been taught this by the father, and that he was sexually abusing the child. She reported him to Child Protective Services.

From the examples given, the reader can see how incidents can get reversed. Do children lie about sexual abuse? Yes, some do with full realization of what they are doing and what the consequences will be for the accused adult. Some do without realizing the seriousness of the accusation or the consequences; to them it is just a story intended to remedy a problem or satisfy a need. Anyone who has worked with or lived around children for any length of time knows that they love to tell "stories"; the more bizarre and scarier the story, the better. Young children frequently become confused as to whether they are telling a story, a dream, something they saw on television or in the movies, or something that has some basis in reality. Children are endowed with a very rich fantasy life and imagination, and can spend hours living in that unreal world.

Currently, some authorities will say that children cannot prefabricate stories about sex and sexual functions unless they have had such an experience. In today's world children are able to experience vicarious sexual experiences on a daily and nightly basis through cable TV and MTV. Even the most conscientious parents, who put their children to bed early and never allow them to watch cable or MTV, cannot control every moment of the child's life—unless they are there every moment. When they go out and leave their child with an adolescent babysitter, that teenager may watch cable and MTV and may not be concerned if the child also watches. Other children who are knowledgable about sex do tell naive children in graphic detail what they know. Children experiment with each other's bodies, trying out what they have been told by other children, or what they have seen in books, magazines, and on television. Children confuse sexual incidents with scary events they have witnessed or heard about; both are part of a forbidden and not very understandable world, and, so, to fuse the two together along with an occasional nightmare is not that uncommon.

The following is an illustration of what has been previously described. The dialogue comes from the author's interactions with two children: a boy, almost 5, and his 7-year-old sister.

GIRL: Want to hear the scary dream I had last night?

SRM: Sure. What was it about?

BOY: I had a scary dream too—first there was—

SRM: Wait a minute. Your sister started first. Let her tell her dream. Then it will be your turn.

GIRL: I dreamed there was this man in a cape and when he turned around he had fangs for teeth—like a vampire—and he was going to bite me and suck my blood all out of my body! Ugh, it was gross!

SRM: My, that is scary. I'll bet you were glad when you woke up. What else did the man look like, besides having fangs?

BOY: I dreamed too—about a vampire but it was scarier 'cause—

SRM: It's not your turn yet. Let's wait until your sister finishes. You were going to tell me about the scary man and what he looked like.

GIRL: He looked like the guy on MTV.

SRM: You get to watch MTV a lot?

GIRL: Not supposed to but when Mom went to the store I watched it with Jill [*adolescent sister*]. In this song, see, this guy is really, I mean really gross looking. He has on a cape and grabs this girl and pushes her to the floor and lays on her and covers them with the cape. I said oh gross—he's sucking her blood. Jill said, No stupid he's screwing her. So I guess he was screwing her—really gross [*nervous laughter*]! In my dream the vampire was going to screw me but I woke up when he was sucking my blood. Yuk! Really gross—huh?

SRM: Sounds pretty scary the way you describe it. What is screwing? Do you know what screwing means?

BOY: I do—screwing is [*screeching laughter*]. My dream is better.

GIRL: Sure. Screwing is when the boy puts his pee-pee in the girl—down here [*points to genitalia*] where you go to the bathroom. God! Really grotty to the max!

BOY: I tried to put my pee-pee in Bubba [*the family dog*]. I got out of the bathtub but he growled and ran away [*screeching laughter*]. My turn. In my dream there was this vampire too—only he had a knife, and fangs, and long claws—but . . . [*draws this out for dramatic effect*] there was another monster too—scarier, with two heads that had fangs and his skin was all peeling off and bloody—and some men had to burn the monster to kill it [*story is told in a very excited and animated way*].

SRM: Is that a dream or a story? Did you see it on TV?

BOY: Its a stor—no my dream I told you! Did you see *The Thing*? Its a monster and it keeps on becoming somebody else and its all bloody looking and they have to burn it so it will die but it doesn't die.

SRM: That's really scary too. Did they finally get rid of *The Thing* so it will not scare any more kids?

BOY AND GIRL: [*They each add parts of the story back and forth*]. No—see they keep burning up people that *The Thing* has turned into—and everybody gets killed—but in the end a dog runs away and *The Thing* is in the dog—so it can go where there is more people. It just keeps living, I guess—so finally everybody in the whole world dies except *The Thing*.

SRM: Well, that was a very scary story. Sometimes it is really fun to tell scary stories. I am glad though it is just a story and not real. The story about *The Thing* doesn't happen in real life; just on TV and in dreams. It must be hard sometimes to remember what is a made-up story, and a dream, and what you see on TV, and things that can happen in real life.

GIRL: Sometimes you wonder if it can happen or if your dreams can come true. Sometimes if I'm walking home from school by myself, I think I see monsters hiding behind trees, or one is following me—and then I run but nothing's there. Its real scary.

BOY: Want to hear another dream I had—its real, real scary!

All teachers who have been around children for some time have had similar experiences. One child in the class tells a story that impresses and gets the others excited; in no time every child wants to be in the limelight and tell better and better stories. In reality, the stories are usually quite similar to the original, but as each child tells the story it becomes more embellished, with a little bit of a different twist here and there. They will all swear it is a true story.

THE DOUBLE-EDGED SWORD

The dilemma that society is faced-with now should be obvious: It is a doubled-edged sword. Some children do lie; some children do tell "stories"; some children do confuse reality with fantasy; some children do know about sex and sexual activity at very young ages and not from direct experience. Some children do become abused in all types of ways; some children do tell the truth about these experiences. Children must be protected as much as anyone else, but innocent adults must be protected too. We have to know *all* of the truths, not just *some* of the truths.

In the past, children were seldom believed when they claimed that they had been sexually abused. That has changed for the most part, and it is now generally accepted that children tell the truth about sexual abuse. Discovering that some children lie, tell stories, and confuse reality with fantasy is one of those truths, but there are serious potential consequences for innocent children who have been abused. We are now in a dangerous position, as more false accusations are discovered. The danger is that we will return to a time past when children were seldom believed. That is one edge of the sword. The other edge is that we cannot continue to allow innocent adults' lives and careers to be destroyed, either. There are no easy answers to this present dilemma. What is needed to solve this problem is an all-out multidisciplinary effort that would include attorneys, educators, psychiatrists, psychologists, physicians, and social workers. All need to work together to establish how our society is going to protect *all* of the innocents.

SELF-PROTECTION FROM FALSE ACCUSATIONS

Not too long ago the author attended a small presentation by a psychologist who had served as an expert witness in a child-abuse case against a teacher. The auditorium was filled primarily with concerned parents and teachers. This psychologist had been a witness for the defense. The teacher originally was found guilty, but later in another court was declared not guilty. After this rather disturbing and stressful presentation, the floor was open to questions from the audience. One teacher in the audience asked the question, "As a teacher, how do I protect myself from something like this happening to me?" The psychologist replied, "Get an attorney." He then went on fielding other questions from the audience. The author felt extreme empathic distress for the teacher who asked that question. Imagine the anxiety the teacher must have been feeling, sitting there knowing that an innocent teacher had spent months in prison because of a false accusation. Keeping a lawyer on retainer, which is very expensive, is not the only means a teacher has to be protected. Retaining an attorney is the last resort to use when false accustions have been made.

In the next section guidelines will be presented in order to *prevent* potential false accusations; the first and most important starting place is prevention. Preventative measures, should they not be entirely successful, will then be part of the educator's protection if a false accusation is made and he or she requires the defense of an attorney.

Protection For Teachers Of Handicapped Children

Because of the current mood of society today, guidelines are necessary for all teachers, and they are *most* essential for teachers of handicapped children.

On a daily basis teachers work with children who require special handling and special techniques that are often misunderstood:

working with severely handicapped children who do soil their clothing and require assistance in cleaning up; or working with emotionally disturbed children who can be very aggressive, who act-out sexually, who live in fantasy worlds, who lie, cheat, steal, and who can be very vindictive and abusive to others; or working with learning-disabled children, who are often frustrated and have learned to fabricate stories to explain away a number of things that bother them; or working with severely and profoundly mentally retarded, autistic children who are self-abusive.

The forms in *Appendix A* were designed not only to help the teacher detect child abuse but are for self-protection also. They are an on-going data base that indicate the conditions of the children who enter at the beginning of the year and what happens to them as they matriculate to the end of the year. It is important to have these forms signed by a witness, such as a school nurse, or principal, who has observed the same signs and symptoms.

Form 3 in Appendix A is particularly useful for children who are self-abusive. These handicapped youngsters usually perseverate in their own abuse: i.e., most will select a certain area of the body and they will scratch, bite, and dig at themselves. Some pull out their own hair. Some are head-bangers and have many bumps and bruises. Seldom, however, do they randomly abuse different parts of their bodies. If the teacher starts on day one using Form 3 with each child, he or she will have an established record of a pattern of the child's own self-abusive behavior. Should anyone question the teacher about such marks on the child, the teacher has a documented record that has been witnessed. If new marks appear in different places that are not within the usual pattern on the child's body, the teacher has a record and probable reason to suspect that someone else might be abusing the child. The forms can be used to indicate new marks; again, have them witnessed. Forms 1 and 2 in Appendix A are essential for teacher-documentation, and form 4 in Appendix A will help the teacher document potentially dangerous events. Do not dismiss the importance of keeping a record of parental behavior. Along with the forms that have been provided in the Appendices, there are a number of actions to take and actions to avoid. These do's and don'ts apply to the teacher's aide as well.

1. *Never* give a child a ride in your car, even in an emergency.

2. *Never* take children on field trips away from the school unless at least two parents are present. Even then, think two or three times before taking children from the school grounds until the hysteria over sexual abuse settles down.

3. *Never* go into a bathroom alone with the children. This applies even if the teacher is a man and the students are boys, or if the teacher is a woman and her students are girls. If children are misbehaving and will not come out of the bathroom, send for the principal, the school nurse, and any other witnesses you can bring along.

4. *Never* touch a child, except on the shoulder or to take them by the hand to lead them to their seats, or wherever it is you want them to be.

5. *Never,* no matter how innocently affectionate and loving, hug, kiss, or pat a child on the bottom, and do not let them give you extended hugs or kiss you even on the cheek. It is not uncommon for older mentally retarded youngsters to greet you with a big bear-hug and a kiss. Teach them how to shake hands and greet people who are not their family members.

6. *Never* tell them any of your personal or private business, such as how much money you make, the type of car you drive, where you live, or that your great, great aunt died and left you 2 million dollars.

7. *Never* let them into your home. Some children will discover where you live and just drop in for a visit. They are never to be allowed to come into your house, where sometime later they would be able to describe the layout, decorations, or rooms.

8. *Never* change a diaper or any other clothing without another adult witness around.

9. *Always* document for your files any false accusation the child makes, such as: "You are mean to me. You hate me."

10. *Always* try to have an adult witness the false accusation of a child. For example, a child in a class for the emotionally disturbed stuffed paper in her knee-high sock and went up to the teacher and said, "See where you kicked me." That child should be taken immediately to the principal, who should be told what the child has just done and said. It should be documented in the teacher's files and signed by the principal. A copy for the principal's file is also suggested.

11. *Always* try to have a parent visit the classroom and help for the day. This can be rotated among parents. Some may put in more time than others, and some may put in no time. Perhaps the teacher will never have a parent in the classroom on a consistent basis, but now more than ever, teachers need to get closer to parents and make more of an effort to work with them. The teacher should meet all of them and see as much of them as possible. The sad fact is that parents have to learn to trust teachers again and they never will unless the teacher insists they get acquainted. There are some preschools where it is a requirement that each parent assist at least 2 days a month or the child cannot attend.

12. *Always* make a big issue in front of the whole class if a child touches the teacher in a place he or she should not. Take the child to the principal and tell what the child did. Document it in the files and have the principal sign as a witness. Send a note home to the parents, with the principal's signature on it, also, stating what their child did and ask that it be signed and returned. Keep a copy of the note sent in the file, in case the parents do not return the original.

13. *Always* take the child immediately to the school nurse if he or she acquires an injury, whether self-inflicted or

accidental. If the nurse is not in the school that day, get another witness to document the report of the incident, and then phone the parent immediately to let them know what happened and ask them to come and take their child home.

14. *Always* make sure severely and mentally retarded youngsters are fully prepared and know how to act before taking them into the community. Make certain that the people they are going to come into contact with [e.g., grocery clerks and restaurant waiters] understand this particular population. They should not be taken into the community if they have to be yelled at or tied to a chair or grocery cart. In the first place, this is not the way people should see the handicapped—that will be their lasting impression of handicapped persons. In the second place, it is these types of behaviors that lead people to believe the teacher is abusing them.

In the beginning the author stressed that the reader would not like what was going to be discussed and is needed for self-protection, and also that there would be actions a teacher would not want to take. These are not only strange times demanding strange reversals in our behavior toward handicapped children, but these are also sad times.

Only a year ago the author would have been the last to tell teachers not to give children hugs or a little kiss on the head if they wanted it—the author has always believed in warm, loving gestures. What is really sad is that it is the handicapped children who seem most to need those warm, caring gestures from their teachers. Many of the *nevers* and *always* listed are some of the practicalities educators have to face now. At one time, for most of the behaviors described, the author would have advised the reader to ignore: but, not anymore! Times are different now and there are dangers that teachers never had to think about before. Unfortunately, teachers have to retrain themselves to be brutally practical.

The Double-Edged Sword Again

Now that many of the readers have been scared half out of their wits, and are most certainly depressed, there is something that may ease the anxiety: Supposing worse comes to worse and a teacher is unjustly accused, even arrested, and has to go to court. The teacher would almost certainly be found not guilty. There will be expert witnesses, who will describe the characteristics of the populations that particular teacher teaches. In nearly all cases these children are judged as incompetent witnesses and their testimony, whether given by them on video tape or recounted by a family member, would be judged unreliable (Yun, 1983). If a teacher has acted in good faith, stuck to these strict guidelines, and kept good records, he or she will be vindicated.

The other edge to the sword is obvious: Who will ever believe our handicapped children when they have really been brutally treated and sexually abused? There will always be children who will never be identified, never be treated, protected, or saved. The major portion of this book focused on the teacher's identifying parents who abuse their children. Now the author has just stated that a teacher is not likely to ever be prosecuted for abuse because no one will believe handicapped children are capable of knowing the truth from a lie, reality from unreality, or fact from fantasy. What the author is now warning of is that there are teachers who will take advantage of this situation, and will abuse helpless children. The final bit of advice for the teacher is that to protect all people, the children and the adults, teachers have to be the watchdogs for their own profession.

APPENDIX A

Characteristics Checklists and Documentation Forms

Form 1: The Child

Child's Name _____

Characteristic	√	Date
Self-destructive behavior		
Apathy, depression, and withdrawal		
Academic failure		
Developmental delays		
Hyperactivity, tantrums, and conduct disorders		
Pseudo-maturity		
Lacks trust and withdraws from touch		
Rigid, compulsive, and disorganized		
Feelings of inadequacy and poor self-esteem		
Role reversal—the child takes care of the parent		
Excessive fantasy		
Fearful and hypervigilant		
Lacks creativity and/or initiative		
Lacks familial attachment		
Gender confusion		
Lacks empathy		
Excessive anxiety		
Oblivious to hazards and risks		
Physical injuries to the genital area		
Sexually transmitted diseases		
Difficulty urinating		
Discharges from the penis or vagina		
Pregnancy		
Fear or aggressive behavior towards adults, especially own parents		

Characteristic	√	Date
Sexual self-consciousness		
Sexual promiscuity and acting-out		
Inability to establish appropriate relationships with peers		
Running away, stealing, and using alcohol or drugs		
Regressive behavior, or any behavior that makes the child look retarded		
Seems to use school as a sanctuary by coming early and not wanting to go home		
Complaints of frequent nightmares		
Indirect hints that child is afraid to go home or afraid of someone in particular at home		
Child seems unduly afraid, especially of parents		
Evidence of repeated serious injuries		
Appears undernourished		
Cries often		
Has a handicapping condition		
Overall poor care		
A sense of being discriminated against in the family		
Fears showing signs of positive, normal behavior		
Moodiness		
Aggressiveness		
Stuttering		
Excessive shyness		
Attempts to buy friendships with gifts		
Excessive guilt		
Enuretic (wetting)		
Encopretic (soiling)		
Excessive masturbation		

Characteristic	√	Date
Overly dependent		
Looks for sympathy		
Lonely, asocial, and joyless		
Friendly but superficial with adults		
Fears being alone		
Continual whining		
Fears new situations		
Hypersensitive to pain		
Excessive fear of failure		
Anorexia nervosa		
Accuses someone of abusing him or her		

From *Abuse and Neglect of Handicapped Children,* by Sharon R. Morgan. ©1987 by College-Hill Press, a division of Little, Brown and Company, Inc. Reproduction of this material for any purpose other than clinical work or training is prohibited.

Form 2: Parents or Significant Caretakers

Child's Name _____

Characteristic	√	Date
Discourages social contact outside the family		
Seems very much alone		
Unable to open-up and share problems with an interested listener		
Appears to trust no one		
Makes no attempt to explain child's most obvious injuries, or gives absurd, contradictory explanations		
Seems detached from the child's problems		
Lack of awareness of seriousness of child's condition		
Complains about own or child's irrelevant problems		
Blames a sibling or third party for the child's injury		
Shows a lack of control		
Delays in child's medical care		
Appears to be using drugs or alcohol		
Ignores child's crying or is extremely impatient		
Has unrealistic expectations for the child		
Indicates he or she was an abused child		
Consistently forgets to pick-up the child from school (abandonment)		
Dresses child inappropriately for the weather		
Describes the child as bad or different		
Appears mentally retarded or immature		
Appears emotionally disturbed (psychotic)		
Gives the child inappropriate food, drink, or medicine		
Inappropriate treatment of child's injuries		

Characteristic	√	Date
Appears cruel and sadistic		
Criticizes, humiliates, and embarrasses child		
Expects child to parent the parent		
Lack of concern for child's education		
inferiority Low self-esteem, self-hatred, and feelings of		
Living in undesirable economic conditions		
Health problems		
Depressed, anxious, hostile, and promiscuous		
Poor social adjustment		
Irresponsible and unreliable		
Family conflicts		
Family acceptance of violence to socialize		
Blames child for family problems		
Does not provide consistent love, acceptance, and praise		
Cold and rejecting		
Views child as a nonperson		
Threatens abandonment as a disciplinary measure		
Marital strife, divorce, death or working mother		
Tries to control the lives of all family members		
Battered wife		

 From *Abuse and Neglect of Handicapped Children,* by Sharon R. Morgan. ©1987 by College-Hill Press, a division of Little, Brown and Company, Inc. Reproduction of this material for any purpose other than clinical work or training is prohibited.

Form 3: Injuries to Child

Child's Name _____ Date: From _____ to _____

Front	Back
Head:	**Head:**
Neck:	**Neck:**
Shoulders:	**Shoulders:**
Arms:	**Arms:**
Hands:	**Hands:**
Torso:	**Torso:**
Genitalia:	**Buttocks:**
Legs:	**Legs:**
Feet:	**Feet:**

Notations:

From *Abuse and Neglect of Handicapped Children,* by Sharon R. Morgan. ©1987 by College-Hill Press, a division of Little, Brown and Company, Inc. Reproduction of this material for any purpose other than clinical work or training is prohibited.

Form 4: Description of Incident

Child's Name _____

Date	Description	Witness(es)

From *Abuse and Neglect of Handicapped Children,* by Sharon R. Morgan. ©1987 by College-Hill Press, a division of Little, Brown and Company, Inc. Reproduction of this material for any purpose other than clinical work or training is prohibited.

APPENDIX B

Toll-Free Hot Line
Numbers

NATIONAL CHILD ABUSE HOTLINE

1-800-422-4453

The National Child Abuse Hotline number is in operation 24 hours a day, 7 days a week. This is the toll-free number to call if you do not find the one you need from the list below that was provided by AT&T Communications. The Hotline will be answered by professional counselors and trained volunteers who can provide help in crisis situations, as well as make referrals to every county in the United States for reporting child abuse. This hotline is a part of the Childhelp USA program and also can assist you in finding sexual abuse treatment programs, shelters, and legal aid.

OTHER 1-800 NUMBERS

Arkansas

Social Services Child Abuse and Neglect
Little Rock, AK 482-5964

California

National Child Abuse Hotline
Hollywood, CA 422-4453

Child Protective Services Butte County
Oroville, CA 824-0902

Child Abuse
Riverside, CA 422-4427

Domestic Violence Crisis Line
Riverside, CA 752-7233

Child Abuse Hotline
San Diego, CA 448-4663

Child Abuse Placement & Protective Service 24 Hour Hotline
San Diego, CA 344-6000

Connecticut

Child Abuse Care Line
Middletown, CT 842-2288

District of Columbia

National Center for Missing & Exploited Children
Washington, D.C. 843-5678

Florida

Abuse Registry Children Disabled Elderly Persons
Tallahassee, FL 342-9152

Indiana

Child Protection Service Child Abuse
Indianapolis, IN 562-2407

Illinois

Child Abuse & Neglect Reporting Children & Family Services
Springfield, IL 252–2873

Child & Family Services Child Abuse Department
Springfield, IL 252–2949

Kentucky

Child Abuse & Neglect Hotline
Louisville, KY 752–6200

Massachusetts

Society for Prevention of Cruelty to Children
Boston, MA 392–6046

Child Abuse & Neglect Hotline
Brookline, MA 792–5200

Child Abuse Hotline
Worcester, MA 922–8169

Maine

Child Emergency Human Services Department
Augusta, ME 452–1999

Michigan

Child Abuse Information Center
East Lansing, MI 942–4357

Harbor Hotline Domestic Violence
East Lansing, MI 292–3925

Mississippi

Child Abuse Hotline
Jackson, MS 222–8000

Missouri

Family Services & Child Abuse Division
Jefferson City, MO 392–3738

Montana

Child Abuse Kiwanis Shodair Help Line
Helena, MT 332–6100

Nebraska

Child Abuse & Neglect Hotline
Grand Island, NE 652–1999

Nevada

Child Abuse Center
Reno, NV 992–5757

New Mexico

Child Abuse & Neglect for Nights & Weekends
Albuquerque, NM 348–3456

New York

Child Abuse & Maltreatment Reporting Center
Albany, NY 342-3720

Domestic Violence Hotline
Woodstock, NY 942-6906

Ohio

Stark County Welfare Child Abuse Reporting Line
Canton, OH 233-5437

Oklahoma

Social & Rehabilitation Institutions,
 Child Abuse Unit of Oklahoma County
Oklahoma City, OK 522-3511

Pennsylvania

Child Hotline Childline
Harrisburg, PA 932-0313

Coalition Against Domestic Violence
Harrisburg, PA 932-4632

Rhode Island

Child Abuse Hotline
Providence, RI 742-4453

Texas

Child Abuse Hotline
Austin, TX 252-5400

Crisis Hotline Abused Families
Longview, TX 441-5555

Virginia

Child Protection Services Division
Richmond, VA 552-7096

Washington

Child Abuse Hotline
Olympia, WA 562-5624

West Virginia

Child Abuse Hotline
Elkins, WV 352-6513

APPENDIX C

Sample Reporting Letters

Sample Letter 1: Report

Oral Report Made To: _____ Date: _____ Time_____

Child's Name: _____ / _____ / _____

Age _____ Birthdate _____ Gender _____

Child's Address: _____ Phone: _____

Person Involved: _____

Address: _____ Phone: _____

Father's Name: _____ Mother's Name: _____

Address & Phone If Different From Child's: _____

_____

_____

Signs & Symptoms: _____

_____

_____

_____

_____

Child's Oral Report: _____

_____

_____

_____

_____

Reporter: _____ Signature: _____

Position: _____

Address: _____ Phone: _____

Winess(es) to Report: _____

Position: _____

Address: _____ Phone: _____

Date: _____Time: _____

Copies: 1. Principal
            2. Counselor
            3. School Nurse
            4. File

Additional Witness(es) To Child's Condition: _____

_____

Address: _____ Phone: _____

From *Abuse and Neglect of Handicapped Children,* by Sharon R. Morgan. ©1987 by College-Hill Press, a division of Little, Brown and Company, Inc. Reproduction of this material for any purpose other than clinical work or training is prohibited.

Sample Letter 2: Report

TO: Agency Person
          Address
RE: Suspected Child Abuse and Neglect
DATE:

Dear _____:

    This letter is to follow-up our phone conversation of (date) at which time I reported the possible abuse and/or neglect of (child's name). (Child) is _____ years of age and resides at (address). (Child) lives with his/her (caretaker) at the same address and can be reached at (phone number).

    Enclosed are observational checklists of the signs and symptoms that concern me and have led me to believe that (child) is an abused and/or neglected child. If I can be of any additional help, please do not hesitate to contact me.

                     Your Name
                     Your Position
                     Address and Phone #

Copies: Principal
           Others As Appropriate
           File

 From *Abuse and Neglect of Handicapped Children,* by Sharon R. Morgan. ©1987 by College-Hill Press, a division of Little, Brown and Company, Inc. Reproduction of this material for any purpose other than clinical work or training is prohibited.

References

Abrahamsen, D. [1960]. *Psychology of crime.* New York: Columbia University Press.

Abram, J.C., & Kaslow, F. [1976]. Learning disability and family dynamics. *Journal of Clinical Child Psychology, 1,* 35–41.

Adams-Tucker, C. [1982]. Proximate effects of sexual abuse in childhood: A report of 28 children. *American Journal of Psychiatry, 139* [10], 1252-1256.

Anderson, L.M., & Shafer, G. [1979]. The character-disordered family: A community treatment model for family sexual abuse. *American Journal of Orthopsychiatry, 49* [8], 436-445.

Andrews, L. [1982]. *Medicine woman.* New York: Basic Books.

Bakan, P. [1971]. *Slaughter of the innocents.* San Francisco: Jossey-Bass.

Baron, M.A., Byar, R.L., & Sheaff, P.J. [1970]. Neurological manifestations of the battered child syndrome. *Pediatrics, 45,* 1023–1024.

Bowlby, J. [1984]. Violence in the family as a disorder of the attachment and caregiving system. *The American Journal of Psychoanalysis, 144* [1], 9–25.

Brandwein, H. [1973]. The battered child: A definite and significant factor in mental retardation. *Mental Retardation, 11*[2], 50–51.

Brant, R.S.T, & Tisza, V.B. [1977]. The sexually misused child. *American Journal of Orthopsychiatry, 1,* 80–90.

Brunnquell, D., Crichton, L., & Egeland, B. [1981]. Maternal personality and attitudes of disturbances of child rearing. *American Journal of Orthopsychiatry, 51* [4], 680–691.

Buddenhagen, R.G. [1971]. Until electric shocks are legal. *Mental Retardation, 9*[6], 48–50.

Burgess, R., & Conger, R. [1978]. Family interaction in abusive, neglectful, and normal families. *Child Development, 49,* 1163–1173.

Caffey, J. [1974]. The whiplash shaken infant syndrome: Manual shaking by the extremities with whiplash-induced intracranial and intraocular bleedings, linked with residual permanent brain damage and mental retardation. *Pediatrics, 54,* 356–403.

Camblin, L.D., & Prout, H.T. [1983]. School counselors and the reporting of child abuse: A survey of state laws and practices. *The School Counselor, 30* [5], 358–367.

Chase, P., & Martin, H. [1970]. Undernutrition and child development. *New England Journal of Medicine, 282,* 933–939.

Child Abuse Prevention and Treatment Act of 1974. Public Law 93–247, U.S.C. 93, Senate 1191 [1974].

Cohen, T. [1983]. The incestuous family revisited. *Social Casework, 64* [3], 154–161.

Colley, K.D. [1978]. Growing up together: The mutual respect balance. In L.E. Arnold [Ed.], *Helping parents help their children* [pp. 46–54]. New York: Brunner/Mazel.

Court, J. [1974], Characteristics of parents and children. In J. Carter [Ed.], *The maltreated child.* London: Priory Press.

Curtis, G.C. [1974]. Violence breeds violence? In J. Leavitt [Ed.], *The battered child: Selected readings.* Fresno, CA.: General Learning Press.

Daniel, J.H., Hampton, R.L., & Newberger, E.H. [1983]. Child abuse and accidents in Black families: A controlled comparative study. *American Journal of Orthopsychiatry, 53* [4], 645–653.

Davoren, E. [1974]. The role of the social worker. In R.E. Helfer, & C.H. Kempe [Eds.], *The battered child [2nd ed.]*. Chicago: University of Chicago Press.

Dean, D. [1979]. Emotional abuse of children. *Children Today, 6* [4], 18–20.

De Francis, V. [1969]. *Child victims of sex crimes*. Denver. The American Humane Association, Children's Division.

De Jong, A.R. [1982]. Sexual abuse of children: Sex, race and age dependent variations. *American Journal of Diseases of Children, 136* [2], 129–134.

Delsordo, J.D. [1974]. Protective casework for abused children. In J. Leavitt [Ed.], *The battered child: Selected readings*. Fresno, CA.: General Learning Press.

deSilva, W. [1981]. Some cultural and economic factors leading to neglect. *Child Abuse and Neglect, 5* [4], 391–406.

Durant, W. [1944]. *Caesar and Christ*. New York: Simon and Schuster.

Durant, W. [1966]. *The life of Greece*. New York: Simon and Schuster.

Ellerstein, N.S., & Canavan, J.W. [1980]. Sexual abuse of boys. *American Journal of Diseases of Children, 134* [3], 255–257.

Ellis, A., & Abarbanel, A. [1967]. *Sexual behavior*. New York: Hawthorn Books, Inc.

Elmer, E. [1967]. *Children in jeopardy*. Pittsburg. University of Pittsburg Press.

Elmer, E. [1977]. A follow-up study of traumatized children. *Pediatrics, 59,* 273–279.

Evoy, J.J. [1983]. *The rejected*. University Park, PA.: The Pennsylvania State University Press.

Famularo, R., Stone, K., Barnum, R., & Wharton, R. [1986]. Alcoholism and severe child maltreatment. *American Journal of Orthopsychiatry, 56* [3], 481–485.

Fontana, V.J., & Schneider, C. [1978]. Help for abusing parents. In L.E. Arnold [Ed.], *Helping parents help their children*. New York: Brunner/Mazel.

Foreman, S., & Seligman, L. [1983]. Adolescent abuse. *The School Counselor, 31* [1], 17–25.

Frodi, A.M. [1981]. Contribution of infant characteristics to child abuse. *American Journal of Mental Deficiency, 85*[4], 341–349.

Galdston, P. [1974]. Observations on children who have been physically abused by their parents. In J. Leavitt [Ed.], *The battered child: Selected readings.* Fresno, CA.: General Learning Press.

Garbarino, J., & Ebata, A. [1983]. The significance of ethnic and cultural differences in child maltreatment. *Journal of Marriage and the Family. 45*[4], 773–783.

Garbarino, J., & Garbarino, A.C. [1984]. *Emotional maltreatment of children.* Chicago: National Committee for Prevention of Child Abuse.

Garbarino, J., & Gilliam, G. [1980]. *Understanding abusive families.* Lexington, MA.: Lexington Books.

Gardner, W.I. [1969]. Use of punishment procedures with the severely retarded: A review. *American Journal of Mental Deficiency, 74*[3], 86–102.

George, C., & Main, M. [1979]. Social interactions of young abused children: Approach, avoidance, and aggression. *Child Development, 50*[2], 306–318.

Giaretto, H. [1976]. The treatment of father–daughter incest: A psycho-social approach. *Children Today, 5*[2], 5–34.

Giarretto, H. [1982]. A comprehensive child sexual abuse treatment program. *Child Abuse and Neglect: The International Journal, 6*[3], 263–278.

Gibbon, E. [1899]. *The decline and fall of the Roman Empire.* New York: Collier.

Gigeroff, A.K. [1968]. *Sexual deviation in the criminal law: Pedophilic offenses.* Toronto, Ontario: University of Toronto Press.

Gil, D.G. [1969]. Physical abuse of children: Findings and implications of a nationwide survey. *Pediatrics, 44,* 857–864.

Gil, D.G. [1971]. Violence against children. *Journal of Marriage and the Family, 33*[4], 637–648.

Gil, D.G. [1976]. Primary prevention of child abuse: A philosophical and political issue. *Pediatric Psychology, 1* [2], 54–57.

Giovannoni, J.M. [1971]. Parental maltreatment: Perpetrators and victims. *Journal of Marriage and the Family, 33*[4], 649–657.

Gordy, P.L. [1983]. Group work that supports adult victims of childhood incest. *Social Casework, 64* [5], 300–307.

Graybill, F.C., & Boesen, V. [1976]. *Visions of a vanishing race.* New York: American Legacy Press.

Greene, N.D. [1974]. Identifying the battered or molested child. In J. Leavitt [Ed.], *The battered child: Selected readings.* Fresno, CA.: General Learning Press.

Hanks, J.R., & Hanks, L.M., Jr. [1948]. The physically handicapped in certain non-occidental societies. *Journal of Social Issues, 4*[4], 11–20.

Hebb, D.O. [1946]. On the nature of fear. *Psychological Review, 53,* 259–276.

Herrenkohl, E.C., & Herrenkohl, R.C. [1979]. A comparison of abused children and their nonabused siblings. *Journal of the American Academy of Child Psychiatry, 18,* 260–269.

Herrenkohl, R.C., Herrenkohl, E.C., & Egolf, B.P. [1983]. Circumstances surrounding the occurrence of child maltreatment. *Journal of Consulting and Clinical Psychology, 51*[3], 424–431.

Howson, R.N. [1985]. Child sexual abuse cases: Dangerous trends and possible solutions. *The Champion, 3,* 6–11.

Institutional Child Abuse: Part two. [1977]. *Human Ecology Forum, 8*[1], Ithaca: New York State College of Human Ecology's Family Life Development Center, Cornell University.

James, H. [1975]. *The little victims: How America treats its children.* New York: David McKay.

Johnson, B., & Morse, H. [1968, March]. *The battered child: A study of children with inflicted injuries.* Denver, CO.: Denver Department of Welfare.

Johnson, D. [1981]. Corporal communication in special education. *The Journal for Special Educators, 17*[4], 352–359.

Jones, J.G. [1982]. Sexual abuse of children: Current concepts. *American Journal of Diseases of Children, 136* [2], 142–146.

Junewicz, W.J. [1983]. A protective posture toward emotional neglect and abuse. *Child Welfare, 6* [3], 243–252.

Justice, B., & Justice, R. [1976]. *The abusing family.* New York: Human Sciences Press.

Kanner, L. [1964]. *A history of the care and study of the mentally retarded.* Springfield, Ill.: Charles C. Thomas.

Karpman, B. [1954]. *The sexual offender and his offenses.* New York: Julian Press.

Kassel, J.B. [1985]. Defining the scope of the due process right to protection: The fourth circuit considers child abuse and good faith immunity. *Cornell Law Review, 70*[5], 940–967.

Kauffman, J.M. [1980]. Nineteenth century views of children's behavior disorders: Historical contributions and continuing issues. *Journal of Special Education, 10,* 335–349.

Kaufman, I., Peck, A.L., & Tagiuri, C.K. [1954]. The family constellation and overt incestuous relations between father and daughter. *American Journal of Orthopsychiatry, 24,* 266–279.

Kavanagh, C. [1982]. Emotional abuse and mental injury: A critique of the concepts and a recommendation for practice. *Journal of the American Academy of Child Psychiatry, 21* [2], 171–177.

Kempe, C.H. [1968]. *The battered child.* Chicago, Ill: The University of Chicago Press.

Kempe, C.H., Silverman, F.N., Steele, B.F., Droegemueller, W., & Silver, H.K. [1962]. The battered child syndrome. *Journal of the American Medical Association, 181,* 17–24.

Kempe, R., & Kempe, C.H. [1976]. Assessing family pathology. In R. Helfer, & C. Kempe [Eds.], *Child abuse and neglect.* Cambridge, MA.: Ballinger Publishing Co.

Kent, J.T. [1976]. A follow-up study of abused children. *Journal of Pediatric Psychology, 1* [2], 25–31.

Khan, M. [1983]. Sexual abuse of younger children. *Clinical Pediatrics, 22* [5], 269–272.

Kinard, E.M. [1979]. The psychological consequences of abuse for the child. *Journal of Social Issues, 35* [2], 82–100.

Kinsey, A., Marin, C., Pomeroy, W., & Gebhard, P. [1953]. *Sexual behavior in the human female.* Philadelphia: W.B. Saunders Co.

Kline, D.F. [1982]. *The disabled child and child abuse.* Chicago: National Committee for Prevention of Child Abuse[1].

Kline, D., & Christiansen, J. [1975]. *Educational and psychological problems of abused children.* [ERIC Document Reproduction Service No. ED 121 041]. Logan, UT: Utah State University.

Koch, M. [1980]. Sexual abuse in children. *Adolescence, 15* [59], 643–649.

Korbin, J.E. [1977]. Anthropological contributions to the study of child abuse. *Child Abuse and Neglect, 1*[1], 7–24.

Lippman, L.D. [1972]. *Attitudes toward the handicapped: A comparison between Europe and the United States.* Springfield, Ill.: Charles C. Thomas.

Lourie, I., & Stefano, L. [1978]. On defining emotional abuse. In M. Lauderdale, R. Anderson, & S. Cramer [Eds.], *Child abuse and neglect: Issues on innovation and implementation. (Vol. 1).* [DHEW Publication No. OHDS 78-30147, pp. 201–208]. Washington, D.C.: U.S. Department of Health, Education, and Welfare.

Lystad, M.H. [1975]. Violence at home: A review of the literature. *American Journal of Orthopsychiatry, 45* [3], 328–345.

Machotka, P., Pittman, F.S., & Flomenhaft, K. [1967]. Incest as a family affair. *Family Process, 6,* 98–115.

MacMillan, D.L., Forness, S.R., & Turmbull, B.M. [1973]. The role of punishment in the classroom. *Exceptional Children, 40*[2], 85–95.

Mahler, M.S. [1968]. *On human symbiosis and the vicissitudes of individuation.* New York: International Universities Press.

Maisch, H. [1972]. *Incest.* New York: Stein & Day.

Maisel, E. [1953]. *Meet a body* [Manuscript]. New York: Institute for the Crippled and Disabled.

Martin, H.P. [1976]. *The abused child*. Cambridge, MA.: Ballinger Publishing Co.

Martin, H.P., & Beezley, P. [1974]. Prevention and consequences of child abuse. *Journal of Operational Psychiatry, 6,* 68–77.

Martin, H.P., Beezley, P., Conway, E.F., & Kempe, C.H. [1974]. The development of abused children. *Advances in Pediatrics, 21,* 25–73.

Martin, H.P., & Rodeheffer, M.A. [1976]. The psychological impact of abuse on children. *Pediatric Psychology, 1* [2], 12–16.

Masterson, J.F. [1976]. *Psychotherapy and the borderline adult*. New York: Brunner/Mazel.

McDaniel, T.R. [1980]. Corporal punishment and teacher liability: Questions teachers ask. *The Clearing House, 54*[1], 10–13.

McMurtry, S.L. [1985]. Secondary prevention of child maltreatment: A review. *Social Work, 30*[1], 42–47.

Meier, J.H. [1985]. *Assault against children*. San Diego: College-Hill Press.

Merrill, E.J. [1975]. Physical abuse of children—An agency study. In: *Protecting the battered child*. Denver, CO.: American Humane Association, Children's Division.

Milner, J.S., & Wimberley, R.C. [1980]. Prediction and explanation of child abuse. *Journal of Clinical Psychology, 36*[4], 875–884.

Monane, M., Leichter, D., & Lewis, D.O. [1984]. Physical abuse in psychiatrically hospitalized children and adolescents. *Journal of the American Academy of Child Psychiatry, 23*[6], 653–658.

Money, J. [1982]. Child abuse: Growth failure, I.Q. deficit, and learning disability. *Journal of Learning Disabilities, 15*[10], 579–582.

Morgan, S.R. [1976]. The battered child in the classroom. *Journal of Pediatric Psychology, 1* [2], 47–49.

Morgan, S.R. [1979]. Psychoeducational profile of emotionally disturbed abused children. *Journal of Clinical Child Psychology, 8* [1], 3–6.

Morgan, S.R. [1984]. Counseling with teachers on the sexual acting-out of disturbed children. *Psychology in the Schools, 21* [2], 234–243.

Morgan, S.R. [1985]. *Children in crises: A team approach in the schools.* San Diego: College-Hill Press.

Morse, C.W., Sahler, O.J.Z., & Friedman, S.B. [1970]. A three year follow-up study of abused and neglected children. *American Journal of Disabled Children, 120,* 437–446.

Moss, S.Z., & Moss, M.S. [1984]. Threat to place a child. *American Journal of Orthopsychiatry, 54* [1], 168–173.

Mrazek, P.B. [1980]. Sexual abuse of children. *Journal of Child Psychology and Psychiatry, 21* [1], 91–95.

Muir, M.F. [1976]. Psychological and behavioral characteristics of abused children. *Journal of Pediatric Psychology, 1* [2], 16–19.

Mulford, R. [1958]. Emotional neglect of children. *Child Welfare, 37,* 19–24.

National Committee for Prevention of Child Abuse. [1983]. *It shouldn't hurt to be a child.* Chicago, Illinois: NCPCA

Nazzaro, J. [1974]. Child abuse and neglect. *Exceptional Children, 40*[5], 351–354.

Nolley, D., Boelkins, D., Kocur, L., Moore, M.K., Goncalves, S., & Lewis, M. [1980]. Aversive conditioning within laws and guidelines in a state facility for mentally retarded individuals. *Mental Retardation, 18*[6], 295–297.

Notes. [1985]. The testimony of child victims in sex abuse prosecutions: Two legislative innovations. *Harvard Law Review, 98*[4], 806–827.

Ogbu, J.U. [1981]. Origins of human competence: A cultural-ecological perspective. *Child Development, 52,* 413–429.

Oliver, B.J. [1967]. *Sexual deviation in American society.* New Haven, CT: United Printing Services.

Otto, M.L. [1984]. Child abuse: Group treatment for parents. *The Personnel and Guidance Journal, 62* [6], 336–338.

Ounsted, C., Oppenheimer, R., & Lindsay, J. [1974]. Aspects of bonding failure: The psychopathology and psychotherapeutic treatment of families of battered children. *Developmental Medical Child Neurology, 16,* 447–456.

Palmer, R.R., & Colton, J. [1967]. *A history of the modern world.* New York: Alfred A. Knopf.

Peters, J.J. [1976]. Children who are victims of sexual assault and the psychology of the offenders. *American Journal of Psychotherapy, 30,* 398–421.

Piele, P.K. [1978]. Neither corporal punishment cruel nor due process due: The United States supreme court's decision in Ingraham v. Wright. *Journal of Law and Education, 7*[1], 1–19.

Powell, G.F., Brasel, J.A., & Blizzard, R.M. [1967a]. Emotional deprivation and growth retardation simulating idiopathic hypopituitarism. I: Clinical evaluation of the syndrome. *New England Journal of Medicine, 276,* 1271–1278.

Powell, G.F., Brasel, J.A., & Blizzard, R.M. [1967b]. Emotional deprivation and growth retardation simulating idiopathic hypopituitarism. II.: Endrocrinologic evaluation of the syndrome. *New England Journal of Medicine, 276,* 1279–1283.

Propst, L.B., & Nagle, R.J. [1981]. Effects of labeling and a child's reaction to punishment in subsequent disciplinary practices of adults and peers. *American Journal of Mental Deficiency, 86*[3], 287–294.

Rohner, R. [1975]. *The love me, they love me not: A worldwide study of the effects of parental acceptance and rejection.* New Haven: Human Relations Area File Press.

Rolston, R.H. [1971]. The effect of prior physical abuse on the expression of overt and fantasy aggressive behavior in children [University Microfilms No. 71-29, 389]. *Dissertation Abstracts International, 32,* 2453B–3086B.

Roos, P. [1974]. Human rights and behavior modification. *Mental Retardation, 12*[3], 3–6.

Rose, E., & Hardman, M.L. [1981]. The abused mentally retarded child. *Education and Training of the Mentally Retarded, 16*[2], 114–118.

Rothstein, L.F. [1985]. Accountability for professional misconduct in providing education to handicapped children. *Journal of Law and Education, 14*[3], 349–393.

Rush, F. [1980]. *The best kept secret.* New York: Prentice-Hall.

Rusk, H.A., & Taylor, E.J. [1946]. *New hope for the handicapped.* New York: Harper & Row.

Sandgrund, A., Gaines, R.W., & Green, A.H. [1974]. Child abuse and mental retardation: A problem of cause and effect. *American Journal of Mental Deficiency, 79*[3], 327–330.

Schecter, M.D., & Roberge, L. [1976]. Sexual exploitation. In R. Helfer, & C. Kempe [Eds.], *Child abuse and neglect.* Cambridge, MA.: Ballinger Publishing Co.

Scheerer, M. [1954]. Cognitive theory. In G. Lindzey [Ed.], *Handbook of social psychology* [pp. 91–142]. Reading, MA: Addison-Wesley.

Schultz, L.G. & Jones, P. [1983]. Sexual abuse of children: Issues for social service and health professionals. *Child Welfare, 62*[2], 99–108.

Shah, C.P. [1982]. Sexual abuse of children. *Annals of Emergency Medicine, 11*[1], 41–46.

Shamray, J.A. [1980]. A perspective on childhood sexual abuse. *Social Work, 25* [2], 128–131.

Sheehy, G. [1984, July 29]. When a child is abused: Are you ready to listen? *The El Paso Times Parade,* pp. 4–6.

Sluyter, G.V., & Cleland, C.C. [1979]. Resident abuse: A continuing dilemma. *American Correctional Therapy Journal, 33*[2], 99–102.

Soeffing, M. [1975]. Abused children are exceptional children. *Exceptional Children, 42,* 126–135.

Souther, M.D. [1984]. *Developmentally disabled, abused and neglected children: A high risk/high need population.* [Publication No. 84-30338]. Washington, D.C.: U.S. Department of Health & Human Services.

Spinetta, J.J., & Rigler, D. [1972]. The child-abusing parent: A psychological review. *Psychological Bulletin, 77* [4], 296–304.

Steele, B., & Pollock, C. [1974]. A psychiatric study of parents who abuse infants and small children. In R. Helfer & C. Kempe [Eds.], *The battered child* (2nd ed.). [pp. 89–133]. Chicago: The University of Chicago Press.

Steinberg, L.D., Catalano, R., & Dooley, D. [1982]. Economic antecedants of child abuse and neglect. *Child Development, 52* [3], 975-985.

Steinmetz, S.K., & Straus, M.A. [1973]. The family as a cradle of violence. *Society, 10*[6], 50-56.

Straker, G., & Johnson, R.S. [1981]. Aggression, emotional maladjustment, and empathy in the abused child. *Behavioral Disorders, 17* [6], 762-765.

Summit, R., & Kryso, J. [1978]. Sexual abuse of children: A clinical spectrum. *American Journal of Orthopsychiatry, 48* [2], 237-251.

Swift, C. [1979]. The prevention of sexual child abuse: Focus on the perpetrator. *Journal of Clinical Child Psychology, 8* [2], 133-136.

Tarter, R.E., Hegedus, A.M., Winsten, N.E., & Alterman, A.I. [1984]. Neuropsychological, personality, and familial characteristics of physically abused delinquents. *Journal of the American Academy of Child Psychiatry, 23* [6], 668-674.

Tilelli, J.A. [1980]. Sexual abuse of children: Clinical findings and implications for management. *New England Journal of Medicine, 302* [6], 319-323.

Trout, M.D. [1983]. Birth of a sick or handicapped infant: Impact on the family. *Child Welfare, LXII* [4], 337-348.

Tyler, N., & Kogan, K. [1977]. Reduction of stress between mothers and their handicapped children. *American Journal of Occupational Therapy, 91* [2], 151-155.

Walters, D.R. [1975]. *Physical and sexual abuse of children.* Bloomington, Indiana: Indiana University Press.

Watson, J.D. [1984, September]. Talking about the best kept secret: Sexual abuse and children with disabilities. *The Exceptional Parent,* 15-20.

Welsh, R.S. [1976a]. Severe parental punishment and delinquency: A developmental theory. *Journal of Clinical Child Psychology, 1,* 17-20.

Welsh, R.S. [1976b]. Violence, permissiveness and the overpunished child. *Journal of Pediatric Psychology, 1* [2], 68–71.

Wherry, J.N. [1983]. Some legal considerations and implications for the use of behavior modification in the schools. *Psychology in the Schools, 20*[1], 46–51.

Whiting, L. [1976]. Defining emotional neglect. *Children Today, 5* [1], 2–5.

Whiting, L. [1978]. Emotional neglect of children. In M. Lauderdale, R. Anderson, & S. Cramer [Eds.], *Child abuse and neglect: Issues on innovation and implementation (Vol. 1).* [DHEW Publication No. OHDS 78-30147, pp. 209–213]. Washington, D.C.: U.S. Department of Health, Education, and Welfare.

Williams, B.G. [1981]. Myths and sexual child abuse: Identification and elimination. *School Counselor, 29* [2], 103–110.

Williams, G.J.R. [1983]. Child protection: A journey into history. *Journal of Clinical Child Psychology, 12* [3], 236–243.

Winks, P.L. [1982]. Legal implications of sexual contact between teacher and student. *Journal of Law & Education, 11* [4], 437–477.

Wolfe, D.A. [1984]. Child-abusive parents: An empirical review and analysis. *Psychological Bulletin, 97* [3], 462–482.

Woodling, B.A. [1981]. Sexual misuse: Rape, molestation, and incest. *Pediatric Clinician of North America, 28* [2], 481–499.

Wright, B.A. [1983]. *Physical disability—A psychosocial approach* [2nd ed.]. New York: Harper & Row, Publishers.

Yun, J. [1983]. A comprehensive approach to child hearsay statements in sex abuse cases. *Columbia Law Review, 83*[7], 1745–1766.

Index

A

Abandonment, 61, 65–66
Accusations, of child abuse
  false, 40–41, 85–100
    reasons for, 88–89
  protection from, 94–100
Aggression
  parental, 64–65
  as symptom of abuse, 36–37, 44,
    62
Alcohol abuse
  by molester, 70
  parental, 59–60
Anger, as symptom of abuse, 36–37,
    47, 62, 65–66
Animals, treatment of handicapped,
    19
Aversive conditioning, 74–81

B

Battered children, 36–38. *See also*
    Physical abuse
Behavior, as sign of physical abuse,
    33–38
Behavior-modification, 74–81
Birth defects, effect of on abuse 18,
    46, 52
  cerebral palsy, 52
Brain damage, due to abuse, 46–47

C

Caretakers, abusive, 26, 34, 86. *See
    also* Parents, abusive; Sexual
    abuse; Teachers, of handi-
    capped
Castration, 16. *See also* Sexual
    abuse
Cerebral palsy, 52. *See also* Birth
    defects
Child Abuse Prevention and Treat-
    ment Act, 25–26
Congenital deformities, versus
    acquired, 20
Corporal punishment, 74–80
  "corporal communication," 77–79
  parental, 58

D

Day-care centers, child-abusive, 75–
    77. *See also* Institutions for
    handicapped; Schools, role
    of in child abuse; Teachers,
    of handicapped
Deformities, acquired and congeni-
    tal, 20
Depression, in abused child, 62, 65
Desertion, parental, 61, 65–66
Down's Syndrome, 81
Drug abuse, parental, 59–60